The
SAN DIEGO RIVER

The
SAN DIEGO
RIVER

Dams, Dikes, Floods and Fights

JOHN MARTIN

THE
History
PRESS

Published by The History Press
Charleston, SC
www.historypress.com

Cover images: The 1916 flood breached the Sweetwater Dam and destroyed the Lower Otay Dam. *City of San Diego Water Department Archive*; construction of the wooden trough required more than 9 million board feet of imported redwood and two years of labor. *From William H. Hall's 1888 State Report*; the transmission pipeline, completed in two phases in 1926 and 1935, conveyed water from the reservoir to the city distributing plant. *City of San Diego Water Department Archive*; the San Diego River rises out of the eastern mountains and flows more than fifty miles through multiple transition zones southwest to the Pacific Ocean. *City of San Diego Office of City Clerk, Archives and Records Management*; the river passes through the rugged confines of Mission Gorge, about fifteen miles from the coast. *City of San Diego Office of City Clerk, Archives and Records Management*.

First published 2023

Manufactured in the United States

ISBN 9781467153461

Library of Congress Control Number: 2022948299

Notice: The information in this book is true and complete to the best of our knowledge. It is offered without guarantee on the part of the author or The History Press. The author and The History Press disclaim all liability in connection with the use of this book.

To my wife, Jane, and mother-in-law, Martha, both forever readers.

CONTENTS

ACKNOWLEDGEMENTS

P articular thanks to Rick Crawford and Derrick Moses at the San Diego Central Library, Gary Van Velzer for reading and editing the manuscript, Eric Duvall and the volunteers at the Ocean Beach Historical Society, the folks at the Helix Water District, Anne Miggins at the City of San Diego Archive and Gary Mitrovich of the Lakeside Historical Society.

I am especially indebted to my history professor daughter Dr. Eliza Martin, who lured me into San Diego water history through her "growth by the gallon" interpretation of the town's perpetual water dilemma.

And big-time gratitude to my hiking, backpacking pal Jeff Pasek (who really should have written the book) for access to materials in the city water archive, for sharing his understanding and knowledge of San Diego's water landscape, his blistering edits and his suggestion, during one of our excursions in the San Diego backcountry, that someone "really should write about the early history of the river."

THE RIVER AND SAN DIEGO'S QUEST FOR WATER

The growth of the city of San Diego was clearly determined
by its water development.
—San Diego Chamber of Commerce Water Committee, 1913

W hen the Mexican government ceded the dusty coastal village of San Diego to the United States in 1848 as a prize of war, the Americans inherited a town that held few secrets. Voyages of discovery and decades of geological surveys uniformly praised the tiny town for its fine climate and land-locked harbor and then criticized it for the capricious nature of the nearby river and the general lack of fresh water.

The residents of the new American possession occupied a sparsely populated outpost clinging to the western extremity of the continental United States that featured a small dirt plaza encircled with wood-frame and adobe homes, some stores and a decaying seventy-year-old Spanish mission on the northern edge of the nearby river valley. While the town lacked many of the essentials of growth, most notably a stable water supply, the ambitious, individualistic Anglos—fueled with economic self-interest, cultural indifference, the passion of Manifest Destiny, a fair share of self-righteousness and the belief that the finest harbor south of San Francisco offered untold maritime potential—stood ready to reinvent their town. The Americans replaced adobe houses with clapboards, tortillas with white bread and the Spanish language with English, but solving the peaceful harbor town's water dilemma proved a more complex endeavor.

In the semi-arid Southwest, where drought was the rule rather than the exception, water was the transformative element. The newly arrived Americans understood that without water, their land had little value and viewed the river that coursed through the adjacent valley as the logical remedy to that dilemma. Indeed, the presence of the river tempted the Americans into the false hope that with ego and idealism, they could use the river to realize their municipal aspirations.

But the ephemeral San Diego River, which flowed virtually on the town's doorstep, proved an elusive resource. Residents celebrated the river when the stream ran steady and smooth and quenched their thirst and watered their crops but then cursed it during the extremes of drought when the stream withered and dried or when the river morphed into a flood-swollen torrent. Historically, Americans viewed rivers as a natural resource that users manipulated for their benefit. But human missteps and nature's refusal to cooperate often altered that circumstance. The San Diego River was no exception. For eighty years, frustrated citizens alternately watched the free-flowing river run dry or spill billions of gallons of floodwater into the sea.

San Diegans have always had a complicated relationship with water. Americans learned what the Native Kumeyaays had experienced for centuries: that the river's intermittent nature made the reliance on surface water an uncertain affair. As a result, in the early American days, San Diego's residents took water where they found it. In a normal winter rainy season, the river flowed, and the townspeople scooped up surface water. When the stream ran dry, they dug holes in the riverbed and inserted wood staved barrels to collect the seepage that pooled up from beneath. Whether it was water from local wells or the shallow groundwater wellsprings dug in the sandy, gravel riverbed, the citizens subsisted on a bucket and barrel collection and distribution system that produced a mixed result both in terms of quantity and quality. Local lore related that citizens were more comfortable using the water for bathing than drinking. A running joke among locals quipped that "we boiled it, we screened it, we boiled it again, and then we drank something else."[1] The Americans quickly learned that the river's alternating character made relying on the river's surface water an uneven venture that trapped San Diego in a growth-to-availability conundrum, or as Dr. Eliza Martin characterized it, a "growth by the gallon" mentality.[2]

The unique juxtaposition of Californians and their endeavors to overcome water shortages has encouraged historians to consider the region's divergent water policies, the resulting internecine battles and the effects of greed and political division. Each of the three new American coastal cities—

In 1848, San Diego possessed a fine harbor and a temporal water source in the river that passed directly in front of Old Town. *San Diego History Center.*

San Francisco, Los Angeles and San Diego—faced serious water issues. The efforts of each town to remedy its water dilemma mirrored the broader western circumstance of water management, but with distinct differences. San Francisco had more rainfall but no nearby sites for storage reservoirs and no river supplying water, so the city created the Hetch Hetchy Reservoir and Aqueduct and tapped water from the Sierra Mountains hundreds of miles to the east. Los Angeles shared the same semi-arid climatic conditions as San Diego and had a river passing through the town, but the surrounding area featured no landforms suitable for dams and reservoirs, so the city built a three-hundred-mile-long aqueduct to access the Owens Valley River. San Diego had a contiguous river fed from the interior mountains and a multitude of potential dams and reservoir sites, but the parochial struggle to reconcile the diverging motives of private interest and municipal need made water development a complicated undertaking.

San Diego was a southwestern coastal town situated in a semi-arid enclave with seasonal and unreliable annual rainfall that fell largely in the eastern mountain catchments. San Diego water historian William Wright identified the area's Mediterranean pattern of uneven seasonal rainfall and

San Diegans relied on river groundwater, surface water and flood and mountain water collected behind river dams. *Author's collection.*

cyclical droughts as the culprits that shaped the unpredictable nature of the river and made water development in Southern California a science unto itself.[3] William E. Smythe—writer, irrigation advocate and pioneer of early twentieth-century western water management—believed that water engineering was the long-term solution to overcoming San Diego's climatic uncertainties. Rather than deferring to nature, San Diego watermen must manipulate the natural environment and manufacture a solution.[4]

Smythe's engineering concepts were particularly adaptable to San Diego County's topography, which featured excellent sites for dams and reservoirs. Into the first decade of the twentieth century, the prevailing philosophy among San Diego water managers centered on the creation of an interlinked hydraulic system using dams and conservation reservoirs to collect and store water. It was a matter of practical environmental determinism—they identified methods and resources, determined costs and applied technical skill.

The resulting proliferation of dams on the county's waterways reflected the efforts of private and municipal agencies to manufacture a solution to the town's water problem. By 1923, civic and private enterprises had placed major dams on all the rivers except the San Diego and made San Diego County the epicenter of international dam building. But despite the dam building surge, the lack of a coordinated community effort left early San Diegans digging and damming and surviving on water from wells and river groundwater purchased from private companies.

William Smythe understood the need for San Diegans to engineer a way to overcome the region's semi-arid conditions. *South Bay Historical Society.*

San Diegans, like most westerners and Californians, passionately adhered to Mark Twain's notion of drinking whiskey and fighting over water. And San Diegans did just that. While private citizens, community leaders and local politicians argued over water issues, they all agreed on the importance of developing the San Diego River, but into the twentieth century, philosophical and technical challenges left the river only marginally exploited. The town's limited financial capacity made the establishment of a municipal water system a piecemeal affair and obligated the reliance on private entrepreneurs to develop local water resources. It was simply more cost efficient for the city to buy water from existing private companies than to assume the indebtedness the fabrication of a municipal system required. Unfortunately, the directors of these private corporations often promised to deliver more water than was at their disposal, which precipitated unreliable service and business failures. By the early 1900s, the town's steadily increasing population and improved financial stability had motivated city planners to pursue a municipal water system based on a strategy of water imperialism. This acquisition campaign formed the basis for a city system but did not include developing the river and ultimately failed to meet the consumption needs of the town.

By 1913, developing the river had moved from a vision to a necessity, but the city still faced substantial challenges. Specifically, the city had to gain legal control of the river and then determine the location for a river dam.

The masonry gravity-arched Sweetwater Dam completed in 1888 was the county's first modern dam and then one of the tallest in the world. *City of San Diego Water Department Archive.*

The situation called for rational thought, the willingness to compromise and public unity—commodities unfortunately in short supply in small-town San Diego. The citizens endured fifteen years in the courtroom before the city won the rights to the river and survived twenty years of heated disagreement and multiple public referendums before finally selecting El Capitan as the river dam site. Then, because the El Capitan site created a reservoir that extended into federal property, the city had to negotiate with the Department of the Interior and reckon with the ethical onus of dispossessing a long-established Native American population. During these years of legal wrangling and disagreement, San Diego's population steadily increased, the town's water supply leveled and the value of water increased.

An era ended with the completion of the El Capitan Dam in 1934. At the dedication ceremony atop the dam in February 1935, the pleas from civic leaders, invited dignitaries and the dedicatory committee to reunite the community revealed the profound sense of division that had pervaded the town over the past twenty years. The dedication culminated San Diego's eighty-year quest for water sustainability and offered a moment of public catharsis. It was a seminal event that marked the end of the community divisiveness, concluded the formative era of San Diego's water development,

Most San Diegans considered the completion of El Capitan Dam in 1934 the answer to the town's ongoing water dilemma. *City of San Diego Water Department Archive.*

permanently altered the characteristics of a free-flowing river, presaged the river's amended connection to the town and portended the introduction of water from external sources.

But it was also a deceptive moment. The result was not a resolution. Most San Diegans believed that the El Capitan project was the final component in the town's water development strategy, but in fact, it was only the next increment. So, while the ceremony marked the conquest of the river and healed the city, the moment did not offer a solution to the town's water dilemma.

Chapter 1

SAN DIEGO'S EPONYMOUS RIVER

This is a river with good sweet water.
—Spanish explorer Sebastian Vizcanio, 1602

After five months at sea in May 1602, Spanish mariner Sebastian Vizcaino navigated his flagship *San Diego* into a protected bay on the northern edge of Alta California. On orders from his superior, Viceroy Gaspar de Zuniga, Vizcaino had cruised north from Acapulco along the Pacific coast in search of possible ports for the Manila Spanish galleons returning from the Far East. Retracing the northern voyage of Juan Cabrillo, Vizcaino entered the landlocked bay Cabrillo discovered and named San Miguel in 1542 and renamed the bay San Diego to honor his arrival on the feast day of San Diego de Alcala. Subsequent Spanish trailblazers and settlers who trekked to the region in 1769 accepted Vizcaino's appellation and applied the name San Diego to the sheltered bay, the new mission and presidio and the river flowing through the adjacent valley.

The 2-million-year-old river antedated human inhabitation and determined the geographical features of the space immediately north of the bay. The river's relentless flow through the east–west corridor carried and deposited unconsolidated alluvial sediment in the riverbed and along the banks, which gradually thickened and elevated the valley floor and formed the flat river basin that is now Mission Valley. The same alluvial action laid down layers of sediment that formed a land bridge that connected the western peninsula to the mainland and formed the mesas that bordered the river valley.

The San Diego River coursed fifty miles from the interior mountain to its outfall into the Pacific Ocean. *Author's collection.*

The San Diego River was at once the most accessible and one of the most remote rivers in the region. The river rose from the streams created from runoff in the valleys and hillsides on the western slopes of the interior mountains in the northeastern backcountry and wound fifty miles to the coast, where it passed within yards of the Old Town settlement. San Diego's earliest American residents knew that the mountain streams fed the river, but only speculated on the river's source. Most believed that the pond known as Cuyamaca, or *Laguna que se Seca* ("Dry Lake"), was the origin. An 1875 account related that the source was in the "northern spurs" near Cuyamaca peak, where runoff and snowmelt created a series of smaller tributary streams that fed into the main river course near Capitan Grande Mountain and then flowed westward.[1] They were essentially correct. Whereas the coastline received perhaps nine inches of rain per year, the east county mountains often experienced between twenty and forty inches during the rainy winter months, feeding the river and its 420-square-mile catchment. Into the 1850s, with no groundwater wells drawing water and no dammed reservoirs on the river, the riparian valleys along the river were undoubtedly wetter, and although periodic flooding scoured out the trees and shrubs and forced the undergrowth to reestablish anew, most likely dense forests of riparian vegetation existed along the major streams and river course. The river's principal tributaries were Coleman, Cedar, Boulder, South Fork and Chocolate Creeks, all of which entered from the east and south above the town of Lakeside. San Vicente Creek, the only important tributary from the north, entered the river near Lakeside.

The river landscape passed through distinctive zones as it flowed out of its fan-shaped watershed on the passage to the sea. The tributary-fed waterway wound through narrow wooded canyons on the upper portion of the river and deposited coarse, sandy, gravelly sediment in the streambed. The river then escaped into the open riparian meadowlands and purled through pine and oak woodlands and chaparral to the halfway point below El Cajon Mountain (popularly called El Capitan Mountain). Here the stream entered a scrub, sage and mixed woodland environment and followed the gentle forested grade into the flat Santee-Lakeside plateau, or the El Cajon basin, before it entered two-mile-long, steep-sided Mission Gorge. After the river flowed between the confined rocky igneous slopes of the gorge, one of the few spots where bedrock surfaced in the streambed and on the surrounding slopes, the water emerged into a broad sandy valley channel that gradually curved south then westward between the two broad mesas that separated the river valley.

Local legend held that the river originated in the runoff from Mildred Falls and the nearby mountain tributaries. *Author's collection.*

Once in the half-mile-wide valley, the river meandered westward through the wide tree-lined river basin, where stands of cottonwood grew along the upper watermark and graceful willows lined the lower banks. Significantly, the sandy streambed of the wide and flat-bottomed valley readily absorbed water into the gravel base, which recharged the valuable underground water basins. The lower riverbed consisted of fine-grained sediment, while muddy silt, which dried into powder in the summers, layered the riverbanks. During the rainy season, the river created multiple channels within the valley but in dry times usually coalesced into a single serpentine runnel. The earliest Americans accepted the Spanish name for the lower valley, *La Canada de San Diego*, which freely translated as the glen or ravine of San Diego. After 1870, locals called this six-mile-long by half-mile-wide floodplain, which contained the ex-mission ranchos and old pueblo lands, Mission Valley. The river terminated in a tidal marsh that formed a swath of coastal wetlands covered with coastal sage and a broad river estuary that exited to the Pacific Ocean.

The river was the lifeblood of the region and drew successive waves of inhabitants to its banks. The Native Kumeyaays, who lived along the river

The river flowed downstream through the tree-lined, narrow river valleys of the upper river. *City of San Diego Water Department Archive.*

and had utilized its waters tens of thousands of years before the Europeans arrived, referred to the river as *japai* or *hapai*, meaning the people's waters. The river was the tribe's only true water source of any permanence. They took surface water when available and survived on groundwater in the dry summer months and in times of drought. The seasonal nature of the river compelled the Kumeyaays to migrate along its banks as the surface water retreated upstream following the rainy winter months. Anthropologist Florence Shipek believed that the cohesive authoritarian organization of the Kumeyaays allowed them to marginally manage the river. They constructed primitive rock weirs across the river channels to capture and conserve the surface water and also to retard the flow and allow the water to seep into the ground and refresh the underground supply. Shipek believed that their water management efforts enhanced the tribe's agricultural and animal husbandry efforts.[2] Larry Banagas of the Barona band of the El Capitan Grande Indians judged that the river was a lifeline for the indigenous people.

The river that sustained the natives likewise became indispensable to the encroaching Europeans. From the 1600s forward, nonnative visitors noted the region's pleasant climate and fine harbor but also commented on the scarcity of fresh water. Although a century separated the voyages of seafaring explorers Cabrillo and Vizcaino, they both entered the bay hoping to replenish their fleet's fresh water supply. On both occasions, the indigenous people directed the adventurers to the river in the broad valley north of the bay. Some sixty years after Cabrillo maneuvered his flagship, *San Carlos*, into the bay, Vizcaino recorded in his 1602 ship's log that his crew followed the direction of the Native Americans and waited until high tide to burrow into the sandy riverbed, where he said they retrieved water.

Like Cabrillo, Vizcaino opined that the river did not appear to offer enough water to support a settlement.

The San Diego River was a typical southwestern watercourse and thus a river of extremes. It filled and flowed and often flooded in the rainy winter months, but in the warm summers, the riverbed, as if unaccustomed to water, absorbed any lingering moisture into its sandy crust and the river disappeared. According to Kumeyaay legend, it was the upside-down river. William E. Smythe likewise observed in his 1908 history of San Diego that once the river arrived in the lowlands, "it sinks into the sand in dry summers, after the curious fashion of California rivers, and disappears from sight."[3] In an 1888 report to Governor R.W. Waterman, State Engineer Hammond Hall noted the river's vicissitudes and explained that as summer approached, the San Diego River shrank until by the middle of July you had to ascend thirty miles up its sandy bed to find any surface water.[4]

From early summer into the fall, the San Diego River was a now-you-see-it, now-you-don't stream. Conversely, during the wet season, when winter rains saturated the interior mountains and produced excessive runoff, the river thrived and often flooded. Depending on the season and circumstances, the mercurial San Diego River could be a ribbon of dust,

The dry streambed meandered through the sparsely vegetated middle river valley, with El Cajon Mountain in the distance. *City of San Diego Office of City Clerk, Archives and Records Management.*

a serene stream or a raging torrent. But no matter the river's condition, it was at the center of San Diego's waterscape.

The destiny of the first settlement in New Spain's aggressive plan for colonial expansion into Alta California rested on the probability of the adventurers finding drinking water. Two northbound overland groups, which Inspector General Jose de Galvez tasked to occupy and settle Alta California, departed the Baja Peninsula in March 1769, one under the command of Fernando Rivera and another under Gaspar de Portolá. The adventurers trekked across the desolate landscape with their respective spiritual guides, Father Juan Crespi and Father Junipero Serra, until the combined bands reunited in San Diego in July. Undoubtedly a Kumeyaay lookout spotted the strangely clothed and bearded men and alerted his people. Undoubtedly the European and the native approached the other with curiosity and suspicion. But neither could have comprehended the profound and lasting changes the meeting would bring.

The fate of the enterprise appeared in jeopardy when the exhausted company of soldiers, trailbreakers, muleteers and missionaries completed their brutal five-month march. The overland party established themselves on a hill just above shore of the bay and awaited replenishment from their seagoing compatriots. The depleted travelers cared for the sick and searched for a water source to support the expedition and the future settlement. The Europeans' timing was inopportune, but fortune favored them. The expeditions arrived in the region's driest season at a time when the river generally flowed at its lowest point or was nonexistent. However, the winter of 1769 must have been a good rain year, for in a letter to Father Palou dated July 1769, Serra mentioned that there was plenty of water available in the nearby river.[5] But that abundance was short-lived.

The accounts of Father Crespi brought the river into the historical narrative. In their search for water, Crespi and his companions followed the slow-running river inland from their camp. But the new arrivals also quickly came to appreciate the vicissitudes of that river. Within days, Crespi observed that the once abundant stream quickly diminished to the point where they could easily walk across it. Some weeks later, Crespi, Father Viscaino, seven or eight soldiers under the command of Pedro Fages and the party's engineer, Miguel Costanso, expanded the search upstream. As the group wandered up the sandy riverbed, Crespi described the profusion of oak, willow, elder and poplar trees, along with wild grape and fragrant Castilian rose bushes that lined the banks of the broad river plain. The men followed the stream to the point where the riverbed narrowed and entered

The river course compressed into the narrow confines of Mission Gorge and then dropped into the wide corridor of Mission Valley. *City of San Diego Office of City Clerk, Archives and Records Management.*

a confined gorge, today's Mission Gorge. Standing in the dry riverbed, with the fragrant dried sage and chaparral covering the steep slopes of the rocky canyon, Crespi undoubtedly sensed the ephemeral nature of the river and the inevitability that the river needed rain from the interior mountains to flow and support the new settlement.[6]

Father Francisco Palou likewise recorded in his journal the presence of a valley with arable land and a sizeable river running through it. Palou wandered the sandy valley and noted that the banks of the river were replete with live oak and cottonwood trees and an abundance of what he called wild cocoba. Palou then explained that the stream diminished from day to day until within three weeks it had stopped flowing and only isolated pools of water spotted the riverbed. A member of the Portolá party, Jose de Canizares, surveyed the area around the San Diego outpost and worried that the fresh water supply in the river was "too uncertain" to support a large settlement. Captain Vincente Vila of the ship *San Carlos* noted that the limited amount of water the crew collected from the river was brackish and generally unfit to drink.[7] At this point, the Kumeyaays' environmental awareness undoubtedly saved the Spanish endeavor.

In the warm summer months, most of the Kumeyaays moved to the higher elevations of the foothills, but some remained along the shores of the bay and banks of the river in small, scattered family groups. It was a fortunate circumstance for the Europeans. These individuals showed the Europeans how to dig shallow wells in the sandy riverbed and retrieve potable water. The future of the new settlement hung in the balance for some nine months as the Franciscan padres cared for the sick, attempted to befriend and convert the natives and survived on river groundwater. Meanwhile, the soldiers and priests anxiously awaited the resupply ship. The last-minute arrival of the relief ship *San Antonio* answered the fathers' prayers, and the precarious Spanish foothold survived. Ironically, the river that helped sustain the indigenous people for millennia now sustained the newcomers who would displace them.

The river's surface and groundwater provided water for the settlement and secured the Spanish march of military and religious imperialism. The Franciscans based the success of their Alta California mission system on the conversion and control of the native inhabitants and the presence of arable land and water to implement Spanish agricultural methods. The padres initiated the first river-related activities with the construction of rudimentary irrigation ditches, or *acequias*, to supply their fields with water. But the river did not benevolently relinquish its natural blessing. Father Palou complained in a 1770s report to his superiors about the lack of water. In a recurring theme, Palou mentioned that the river was full one year, flooded one year and dry the next. In a 1772 account on the status of the Mission San Diego, Father Palou reported to his superiors that the river destroyed the grain the fathers had planted in the nearby riverbed. When the priests moved their fields away from the riverbed the next year, the crops died from drought, and the priests were forced to dig wells in the riverbed to secure water for themselves and their animals.[8] Four years of survival along the irregular stream revealed the river's true nature and motivated Viceroy Bucareli, the head of the Spanish colonial government in Mexico City, to instruct Serra in December 1773 to seek a new location for the mission, one with better water and soil.

As the soldiers and missionaries struggled to establish their respective institutions, the new residents offered occasional recollections of the river. Some reminisces were mundane. Father Pedro Font noted in his diary that during the rainy season of January 1776, Captain Juan de Anza dispatched a relief pack train to assist the settlers in San Gabriel, but an overnight downpour caused the river to run so rapid and so deep that he was forced to delay the expedition's departure. Others bore more unrealized significance. In 1773, Father Palou noted that his superiors in Mexico City designated the waters of the river for the "common benefit of all the natives, whether Gentile or converted, who dwell today or in the future in the province" and should be held for the "children and their children and successors for all time forever." Julio Ramon Mendoza, secretary to the viceroy, reiterated to Father Serra that the waters of the stream running through San Diego were for the common benefit of all the people residing there now and in perpetuity.[9] About 240 years later, a San Diego city attorney would argue this point in a courtroom as the city sought to claim the paramount rights to the waters of the river.

Curiosity and the evident importance of the river prompted some of the earliest American explorations of the river. U.S. Army Major E.R.S. Canby, who arrived in California in 1849 as a member of the government's transition team, took the time to wander the river valley from Old Town to the Old Mission Dam. From his outings, Canby noted that the old dam and aqueduct were in good condition and offered his opinion that the river could supply enough water to perhaps support a population of three hundred to four hundred people. Four years later, in March 1853, topographical engineer Lieutenant George H. Derby, in San Diego on a government project to turn the river flow away from the harbor, explored the river to its source and created a descriptive missive entitled the "Memoir of the San Diego River." From his investigations, Derby postulated that the tributary-fed river rose some forty miles east out of a small alpine lake in the mountains that separated the Pacific Ocean and the Colorado River drainages. The young engineer described the sparse forests and shrubbery that lined the low riverbanks and observed that overall the bed of the river was generally of light drifting sand and featured a smooth alluvial bottom. In the report, he also described the fertile soil of the adjacent bottomland, which he speculated offered excellent pasturage and was ideal for agricultural purposes.

Derby also interviewed longtime residents to re-create a description of the river at the time of Spanish arrival. From the conversations, Derby learned that the river valley above Old Town supported a dense forest of sycamore, willow and cottonwood trees and that the brushy undergrowth included wild grapes. He also heard how the constant flow of river sediment had gradually formed the existing sandy plain below Old Town and spread across the river's outfall into False Bay. From local legend, he

Trees and shrubbery lined the river where it departed the restricted valley below El Cajon Mountain. *City of San Diego Office of City Clerk, Archives and Records Management.*

concluded that in the early nineteenth century, False Bay was deep enough to accommodate moderate-sized vessels, but the relentless flow of sediment enlarged the shoals and sandbars; by the 1850s, the bay did not contain enough water to float an ordinary sailboat. Appropriate to his project, the engineer learned that after the heavy storms of 1825, the river developed two distinct channels, one that emptied into False Bay and the other that veered south and carried tons of silt into the harbor.[10]

Professional engineers also surveyed the river. In 1888, State Engineer Hammond Hall delineated the distinctive segments of the river. Like his predecessors, Hall described how the tributaries in rocky mountain canyons of the upper river fed and converged into a single channel that entered the flatlands of the El Monte/El Cajon basin and then moved through the confines of Mission Gorge and into the board valley that funneled into False Bay and the sea. Hall postulated that if the river maintained its perennial flow, ranchers could irrigate the valley with water from the river. With the eye of the engineer, Hall opined that the river course also featured several ideal dam sites for storage reservoirs.[11] Civil and hydraulic engineer Clarence S. Alverson, who had studied the surface and groundwater supply of the river since 1886, offered his view of the river in a 1917 report. In the

The San Diego River Valley stretched from below El Cajon Mountain west to Mission Gorge. *City of San Diego Office of City Clerk, Archives and Records Management.*

report, Alverson recorded a detailed geological survey of the river below El Cajon Mountain and wondered whether the city would ever build a dam on the site.

Human intervention after the turn of the twentieth century exerted tangible changes on the river. Ranchers and dairy farmers clear-cut trees and burned away underbrush along the riverbanks for fuel and shelter and to create usable acreage, permanently altering the river environs in Mission Valley. Quarrymen worked the arroyos west of Mission Gorge, extracting sand and gravel, constantly redirecting the river's course. In the interior of El Cajon Valley, the agriculture-based towns of Lakeside and Santee grew alongside the river and supported ranchers and farmers who took surface water from the river and sunk wells and pumped water from the gravel riverbeds. When coupled with the natural action of the river and periodic floods, these unnatural alterations of the environment irreversibly changed the nature of the terrain surrounding the river and constantly reconfigured the interior channels and external boundaries of the river basin. The various transportation and railroad bridges constructed in the 1880s and 1890s in

Lakeside, Mission Valley and over False Bay were artificial obstacles of small consequence that the river damaged or destroyed in flood events.

The actions of the U.S. government imprinted the river when President Ulysses S. Grant established the Capitan Grande Indian Reservation via an executive order in 1875. The reservation, administered through the Department of the Interior, occupied the eastern slope of the upper San Diego River Valley and limited development along the upper half of the river. When San Diego water interests considered El Capitan, which straddled the federal lands, as a viable dam site, Indian Affairs officials initially opposed the project, asserting that the resulting reservoir would flood reservation lands. Eventually, the pervasive mantra of municipal need for the public good persuaded the department policy-makers to alter their stance, and in 1919, they passed legislation that transferred the river water rights and the adjacent land to the City of San Diego and permitted the city to dam the river.

Chapter 2

FLOODS ON THE RIVER

Floods on the San Diego River are sudden and severe.
—California State Department of Water Resources Report, 1917

As the Americans developed the town and pondered ways to capture the river waters, nature periodically exerted its influence on the river. Location and climate dictated San Diego's variable rainfall, which resulted in climatic patterns that featured seasons where the San Diego River smoothly flowed with natural runoff, went dry during the years of oppressive drought or exploded with devastating effect in unusually rainy years. Floods on the river were generally brief, cyclical, dramatic and impactful episodes, most often rose from an excess of rain falling on the western slopes of the eastern mountains, but occasionally, as in 1861 and 1916, an abnormal condition called an atmospheric river—a narrow corridor of concentrated moisture in the atmosphere—created a deluge that overflowed the river. Between 1887 and 1935, San Diego experienced an average annual rainfall of 9.83 inches, with intervals of abnormally high rainfall that produced a significant flood event approximately every eleven years.

The San Diego River was topographically perfect to produce dynamic floods. Following a significant rain event in the mountains, the accumulated runoff and tributary flow burst out of the arroyos of the upper valley canyons and inundated the flat, shallow agricultural lands of the towns of Lakeside and Santee, gathered momentum as it compressed through the

When the river stormed through the broad interior river valley near Lakeside, it destroyed farms and structures in its path. *City of San Diego Water Department Archive.*

narrow confines of Mission Gorge and then surged into the broad, natural floodplain of Mission Valley. Once in Mission Valley, the shallow variegated river channels were simply incapable of curbing the surging flow as it swept through the river mouth estuary and on to the sea.

Floods in the early American San Diego were a contradiction. As destructive as a flood might be, San Diegans nevertheless depended on these periodic events to augment the river's natural runoff and replenish its groundwater. With the pressing need for water and the erratic incidence of floods, by the 1880s engineers had designed dams on San Diego County's major rivers primarily to conserve floodwater for domestic and irrigation uses, with flood control a secondary goal. For the drought-conscious inhabitants, these floods were also a graphic reminder of wasted water. Into the 1930s, dams on the San Dieguito, Sweetwater and Otay Rivers conserved and captured floodwaters, but for decades frustrated San Diego citizens watched billions of gallons of floodwater spill unrestrained down the San Diego River into the ocean.

The storm of 1811 was San Diego's first recorded rain-flood event, with the next significant episodes coming in the 1820s. The September 1821 flood was unusual in that the Old Town residents had no warning of

Reaching Mission Valley, floodwaters routinely swept away the road and rail bridges that spanned the valley. *City of San Diego Water Department Archive.*

the storm's arrival. The event was truly a flash flood. The storm dropped massive amounts of rain in the interior mountains but deposited little if any precipitation on the coast, which left the residents of Old Town unprepared for the wall of water that cascaded down the river valley that sunny day. The floodwaters washed away the crops and vineyards in the inland *rancherias* and, according to local legend, also swept hundreds of ripe pumpkins from the farms in the Cajon Rancho downstream into False Bay.

The 1821 flood exerted effects that reached into the American era. The strength of the flood created a wall of silt along the river's south bank, away from its natural path into False Bay, and forged a new channel through the river's southern bank near Old Town into San Diego Harbor. The prodigious amount of alluvium the river spewed through the new outlet into the bay over the next twenty-five years threatened the port's utility and initiated the town's first river project. Fortunately, the 1821 flood was a short-lived event, and within two days, the river returned to near normal flow. Typical of San Diego's bizarre weather patterns, the flood marked the beginning of a decade-long drought. Periodic flooding over the next forty years caused localized disruption, but the 1861–62 event was epic.

According to the San Diego Weather Bureau and local recollection, the flood of 1861–62 was the most impressive in memory. With storm prediction essentially nonexistent, the event caught San Diegans totally unprepared. Statewide newspapers referenced that rain fell like a tropical deluge and created the Great California Flood. In this rare atmospheric river storm, cold northwesterly winds pushed a chain of four winter storms down the Pacific coast, one after the other, for almost four months. The rain started in November 1861, fell every day in January and continued intermittently into May 1862. The overflowing river forced residents to evacuate Old Town and flee up nearby San Diego Mesa for safety. Mission Valley was underwater. In San Diego, as the rest of Southern California, this so-called Noachian Deluge washed away houses, orchards and stands of trees and engulfed the roads and bridges in the river valley. The flood also razed much of the grazing grasslands in the river valleys, which impacted the region's cattle ranchers. To further torment the rain-soaked citizens, a powerful ocean surge coupled with the unusually high tides backed the storm waters up into the river course, scoured and enlarged the existing channel and forged another waterway into the northern edge of San Diego Bay. The 1862 occurrence was less destructive only because San Diego had fewer than eight hundred inhabitants, most living south of Old Town, and because Mission Valley was only marginally improved and sparsely populated. Aside from the destruction of the remnants of Derby's Dike, the damage was negligible. True to form, three years of harsh drought followed the flood, and no significant rain returned to San Diego until the 1870s.

Over the next two decades, mountain rainstorms precipitated notable river floods, which, as usual, largely affected the developing middle river rural communities of Lakeside and Santee and the farmers in Mission Valley. In 1873, the San Diego River again barreled out of the mountains into the lower populated areas. This was the wettest August on record, and the tropical storm that spawned the episode dropped nearly three inches on Cajon Ranch in one day. The overflowing river forced the use of ferries to continue mail service outside the town. An event in 1890 severed railroad lines, toppled telephones poles, cut the railroad track that crossed the river, nearly washed out the iron wagon river bridge at Old Town and threatened the county hospital and poorhouse in Mission Valley. The storm whipped the ocean into such turbulence that cargo ships could not enter the harbor and offload supplies, which caused a brief food shortage. Locals felt isolated from the rest of the world. But in typical fashion, within two weeks the river

The flood of 1905–6 ravaged Mission Valley and lasted from the winter of 1905 into the summer of 1906. *San Diego History Center.*

had receded, residents cleaned up the town, life returned to normal and the region entered another dry period.

The flood of 1905–6 bookended the brutal drought that extended from 1897 to 1904. The drought was the most severe of the previous ninety-six years, and virtually no river water flowed past Mission Gorge in that time. The flood in the winter of 1905–6 punctuated the end of the drought. The river raged though Mission Valley, destroyed farms and again washed out the northern embankment of the Old Town Bridge. This event was peculiar for its duration, which extended through the winter and into the summer of 1906. Because the floods of the 1870s and 1880s had swept away trees and brush growing along the banks and on the river's interior sandbars, these storm waters flowed with excessive pace.

Into the first decade of the twentieth century, San Diegans accepted and endured floods as a part of the river's ethos. But fortunately, these flood events struck when the river basins in Mission Valley and El Cajon Valley were sparsely populated. But as the town grew, so did the possibility of greater loss. Between 1900 and 1910, the town more than doubled its population, and by 1915, the town contained nearly forty thousand residents. Likewise, more farmers, ranchers and their animals and structures occupied Mission Valley and the river valley that extended from below El Cajon Mountain to Mission Gorge. So, as San Diego grew, the prospect of increased damage

In 1916, the city hired the self-proclaimed "rainmaker" Charles Hatfield to fill local reservoirs. *South Bay Historical Society.*

and displacement proportionally increased. The time was right for disaster, and the 1916 event became a benchmark flood and a true memory maker.

The flood of 1916 was unique for more than just the weather. The winter of 1914–15, the only wet season in the previous seven, did little to mitigate the suffering of an extended drought that started in 1910. Eager to entertain any promise of drought relief, the parched citizens of San Diego intersected with Charles Hatfield, a self-proclaimed "moisture accelerator," in the winter of 1915. For $10,000, Hatfield guaranteed to fill the city's Morena Reservoir, located in the remote southeastern corner of the county, which in 1915 sat nearly empty. Hatfield faced a formidable task. Since the dam's completion in 1912, the 15-billion-gallon reservoir had never filled to capacity. The Common Council debated Hatfield's proposal; then, with a 4-1 vote and the approval of Mayor Edwin Capps, it ordered City Attorney Terence Cosgrove to fashion a contract. For whatever reason, Hatfield never signed the contract but nevertheless set to work.[1]

Hatfield established himself above the slopes of Morena Reservoir, mixed his potions and dramatically released the chemical concoction into the air. Charlatan or not, within days the rains began and ultimately unleashed one of the worst flood events in city history. As in 1861, this was an atmospheric river phenomenon. The rain started on January 5, continued for five days and increased in intensity on the tenth; on January 27, the San Diego, the Tijuana and the Otay Rivers overflowed. That January 1916, San Diego received twenty-eight inches of rain, far more than double the town's typical annual total.

The county's drought-depleted rivers raged westward with a fury. The Tijuana River wiped out William Smythe's Little Landers agricultural community and breached Sweetwater Dam. The Otay River rose twenty-seven feet in ten days, damaged the Sweetwater Dam and overtopped and totally destroyed the Otay Dam. In Otay Valley, the surge from the destroyed reservoir swept away ranches, farms and livestock in the valley and took the lives of an estimated twenty to thirty people. The flood surge of the San Diego River struck Mission Valley, washed out the city's river groundwater wells, collapsed the concrete highway bridge and the railroad bridge, razed the telephone and telegraph transmission lines, swept away the distribution routes of the San Diego Consolidated Gas & Electric Company between El Monte and False Bay and separated the city from the communities on the northern side of Mission Valley. The swollen river that swept through Lakeside destroyed twenty-one homes; submerged farms and ranches; collapsed water towers, barns and assorted outbuildings; and demolished the Lakeside Bridge along with six miles of the Cuyamaca Water Company's flume line.

Tangentially, the 1916 flood reignited the smoldering feud between the citizens of San Diego and Los Angeles. The *Los Angeles Times* reported that the floodwaters of the San Diego River had heavily damaged downtown San Diego, destroyed the city's water supply and left the citizens "up to their necks in water." The *San Diego Union*, of course, blasted the *Times* reports as greatly exaggerated and exhorted the public to discount the "maliciously distorted accounts."[2] The San Diego Chamber of Commerce called on Mayor Edwin Capps and the Common Council to take steps to

The 1916 flood breached the Sweetwater Dam, show here, and destroyed the Lower Otay Dam. *City of San Diego Water Department Archive.*

refute the reports and dispatched a delegation to Los Angeles to explain the true conditions and reassure commercial organizations that San Diego was open for business. The episode dovetailed into a massive citywide letter writing campaign directed at the citizens of Los Angeles to protect San Diego's image.

While the respective newspapers waged a war of words, city officials and Hatfield skirmished over indemnity and payment. Hatfield met his obligation. Indeed, the storm supplied more water than he promised. But the city refused to pay the bill. Hatfield filed a $10,000 suit against the city to recover his costs. When that action stalled, Hatfield eventually offered to accept $4,000; with no response, Hatfield asked for $1,800 for his time and expenses. City Attorney Terence Cosgrove agreed to pay Hatfield if he accepted responsibility for the $3.5 million in damages filed against the city. Hatfield's attorney purportedly told Cosgrove to go to hell. The Common Council naturally backed Cosgrove's insistence that the city was not obligated to compensate Hatfield. In lieu of compensation, Hatfield earned the reputation as a rain expert and garnered requests for his services in other drought-stricken areas. The case remained in the court system for twenty-two years before a San Diego judge dismissed the case for lack of prosecution in 1938.[3]

The 1916 flood destroyed several bridges and the trolley lines that ran through Mission Valley. *Ocean Beach History Society.*

On a broader scope, the wide-scale statewide flooding and devastation of 1916, and the failure of the Otay Dam specifically, prompted the State of California to initiate new safety and regulatory measures for dam construction. From this point forward, the state engineer and the California Railroad Commission supervised construction of any structure in irrigation districts and at all public utility dam projects.

The next episodic flood event occurred in 1927, in what was the heaviest rainfall since 1916. Two huge storms struck the county in mid-February and dropped seven inches of rain on the city. Citizens feared that it was a repeat of 1916. The storm filled city streets, ripped away telephone poles and railway tracks, swept away two bridges on the San Diego River, inundated the El Cajon Valley, destroyed Lakeside's water supply, submerged the roads crossing Mission Valley and turned the lower San Diego River basin into a single huge lake. The rising water isolated the town for several days, with the only access via boats or airplanes. Unlike the event of 1916, all the major dams in the county escaped major damage. On the positive side, the storms dumped an estimated 65 billion gallons of water into the local reservoirs at Barrett, Morena and Otay. With no major flood control or collection

In 1927, the river overflowed into the outer edges of Lakeside, destroying farms and the single wooden road bridge that spanned the river. *Lakeside Historical Society.*

structure on the San Diego River, San Diegans could only repair the localized destruction and lament the loss of additional billions of gallons of water.

The specter of periodic river floods prompted increased public concern as the region's population grew, specifically the inland communities of Santee and Lakeside, and the spread of the San Diego municipal area into Mission Valley. Community leaders also remained focused on the volume of water that poured into the ocean rather than the city's water supply. San Diego's citizens, politicians and water officials stood ready to harness the river to their benefit, but that meant constructing a large dam somewhere on the San Diego River. Into the 1920s, advocates for a river dam argued that delaying the project cost the city billons of gallons of lost water plus the cost in flood damage. Almost universal community sentiment and conviction existed to construct a dam; however, the unforeseen division over where the city would locate a river dam obfuscated any coordinated civic action.

On the eve of the construction of El Capitan Dam in March 1932, California State Engineer J.W. Ferguson produced a report that presciently opined that in a major flood event the El Capitan Reservoir would probably fill within thirty hours and that because of its location on the middle river, it offered little protection against downstream flooding.

In San Diego's formative years, between 1850 and 1934, major floods were a natural decennial occurrence that altered the river's physicality; affected the lives of river valley dwellers through damage, destruction and often death; and were a constant reminder of wasted water.

Chapter 3

LEVEES ON THE RIVER

The levee as a work of so much importance, preserving from utter destruction one of the finest harbors on the Pacific coast, should, when done, be done thoroughly.
—*U.S. Topographic Engineer Lieutenant George H. Derby, 1853*

The first river-related effort of San Diego's new American residents was one of preservation. The ambitious Anglos assumed control of San Diego in 1848 with grand visions and by mid-1850 had incorporated the town, elected a mayor, started a weekly newspaper, convened the local court and introduced the Fourth of July. They also visualized the maritime potential the protected harbor offered. Unfortunately, navigating the channel into the harbor to conduct trade was no easy task for sizable vessels. Inbound ships had to pass over a shallow outer bar that spanned the narrow entry channel and then negotiate an extensive, constantly reconfiguring elliptical sand shoal that traversed the channel between Ballast Point and the Coronado Peninsula. With a shallow-draft vessel and cooperative tides, adroit seamen could manage these navigational hazards. But in addition to these nautical pitfalls, a troublesome natural problem lurked within the bay's interior waters, one beyond any navigator's ken and one that threatened the harbor's integrity and the town's future.

Geologists surmise that over the course of time, as the river transported its sediment-laden waters westward to the ocean, it eventually infused the small sound at the river mouth with so much sand and silt that it became worthless as a harbor. The Spanish aptly named the lagoon False Bay. But while useless

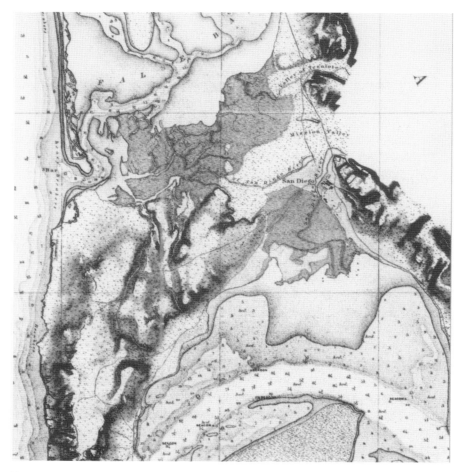

Contemporary U.S. Coastal Survey maps revealed the growing delta of river sediment that encroached into the inner harbor. *San Diego Public Library Map Collection.*

as a harbor, False Bay was the perfect receptacle for the outfall for the river's runoff water, sand and flotsam. In years of normal rainfall, the river did just that. But during a storm event in the 1820s, the flood-driven river escaped its natural channel and turned southward (essentially through today's Marine Corps Recruiting Depot), and the silt-laden flow inundated the northern reaches of the bay and gradually formed a sandy, glacier-like delta. Now, in a quirk of geological irony, the San Diego River, an instrument in the formation of the harbor, appeared on the verge of becoming the instrument of its destruction. This ever-expanding alluvial action threatened to suffocate the upper bay and restrict maritime traffic into the port.

False Bay was the perfect collection point for the massive amount of river-born flotsam and sediment that flowed down the river. *Ocean Beach Historical Society.*

Citizens and experts agreed that, left unchecked, the river's encroachment portended dire circumstances for the new residents and their fledgling town. When U.S. Topographic Engineer Major William H. Emory, an officer with Stephen W. Kearny's American Expeditionary Force, passed through San Diego in 1846, he noted the situation and surmised that the river could eventually destroy the harbor. The officers of the U.S. Coast Survey of 1850 confirmed Emory's opinion.[1] Given the importance of the harbor, San Diego's new citizens took Emory's advice to heart.

THE LEVEE OF 1853

With the river flowing into the bay and the utility of the port in jeopardy, in September 1850 the San Diego Board of Trustees passed an ordinance that authorized $1,000 to build a "pile dam" to turn the San Diego River back into False Bay. But the project was simply beyond the resources of the tiny town. The well-intended scheme languished from a lack of funds and public disinterest, and the trustees soon abandoned the venture. At this moment, a champion, in the form of the U.S. government, intervened.

In late 1850, the U.S. War Department ordered Alexander Bache, the supervisor of the U.S. Coast Survey, to conduct a series of coastal investigations that included an examination of San Diego Harbor. From his inquiry, Bache surmised that if the course of the San Diego River into the bay remained unchanged, the accumulation of sediment would fill and ultimately destroy the harbor for future use. The warning and the government's tacit recognition of the harbor's potential spurred Congress into action in the summer of 1852.

That August, the 32nd Congress funded $30,000 through a Rivers & Harbors Act to construct a levee to redirect the wayward river channel back into False Bay.

With the appropriation approved, Secretary of War Jefferson Davis authorized the chief of the U.S. Topographic Engineers, John J. Abert, to undertake the project. Abert duly assigned Lieutenant George H. Derby, already in Northern California on army business, to travel to San Diego and investigate the diversion project. Derby's assignment was noteworthy as the first federally funded project the Topographic Corps attempted west of the Mississippi River. Derby, a known practical joker (one prank that involved peacock feathers and parade hats almost ended in a court-martial), was already somewhat of a controversial figure in the army, which prompted Derby's fellow officers to wonder if his superiors sent him to San Diego, the "most out of the way" location in the United States, because he was the best engineer for the job, the engineer closest to the site or because they "couldn't stand him."[2] Whatever the circumstances, San Diego had a project and an engineer. The thirty-year-old Mexican-American War veteran arrived on the steamer *Northerner* in the summer of 1852, established his headquarters in Old Town in the Pendleton House and went to work. Derby walked the river valley near Old Town to determine the physical problems the project entailed and then conducted background interviews with longtime residents to gain an understanding of the river's history.

In 1853, John J. Abert, chief of the Topographical Corps, approved the plan to construct a river levee. *West Point Museum Collection, United States Military Academy.*

While Derby set about formulating a plan to block the river from the bay, the brash young officer also had the opportunity to display his literary bent, with the river project his favorite topic. Shortly after Derby's arrival, John J. Ames, the editor of the *San Diego Herald*, befriended him, and for the next three years, he allowed Derby to pen humorous and satirical pieces for the paper through his pseudonym, John Phoenix. When Ames interviewed him, Derby quipped that he was under orders from the "U.S. Hypothetical Engineers" to build a levee to keep the river's "slickens" out of the bay. When asked how the river project was progressing, Derby roundly "denied requisitioning a lathe with which to turn the river" and jested that the army sent him to dam the river and had done so several times since his arrival. As a compliment to the obviously likable Derby, his workers named their riverside shanty camp "Hotel Phoenix." Fortunately, Derby took time between bouts of literary banter to tend to his engineering duties.[3]

Derby initiated the project with a survey of the river with the assistance of fellow engineer Charles. H. Poole, his former West Point roommate and a future San Diego county surveyor, who had accompanied him to San Diego. The young engineers worked under the guidance of prominent local rancher Jonathan J. Warner. Derby examined the flow of the river and postulated that constructing a massive dam spanning Mission Valley, rather than a smaller structure on the sand flat paralleling the river near Old Town, was the optimal solution. After consideration, the ambitious engineer conceded that a larger dam required a more extensive survey and dictated a more complex and expensive project than the Corps intended, and Derby reluctantly abandoned the grandiose idea.

The consequence of Derby's topographic study was a map titled *The San Diego River and Vicinity with a View to the Construction of a Levee and Canal*. The map illustrated the river's path into the bay and the main channel that flowed into False Bay and noted that the riverbed lay about fifteen feet below Old

Town, a measurement that influenced the overall height of the proposed levee. Derby indicated which of the numerous channels carried water and which consistently remained dry. He delineated the river valley's extensive alluvial fan and associated deltas, marshes and mud flats spreading east from Point Loma to the point where the river entered the bay that locals called Dutch Flat.

Derby used the data from his investigations and illustrative map as templates to formulate several proposals. One plan described a simple bulkhead supported with piles that closed the river channel that ran into the bay. Another called for excavating a trench from Presidio Hill to Point Loma and driving a series of thirty-foot-long redwood piles sheathed with diagonal three-inch planks into the riverbed to curb the river. A

Lieutenant George Derby arrived in San Diego to survey and construct a levee to stop the river from flowing into the bay. *West Point Museum Collection, United States Military Academy.*

third scheme suggested a levee, really a dam, with an 8-foot crest and a ditch running along the side facing the river. His final proposal, at $23,253 the only plan within his assigned budget, called for a 1,600-foot levee supplemented with a 20-foot-wide ditch paralleling the river valley. Each scenario called for a barrier faced with a ditch on the bay side of the structure that extended across the sandy flats near Old Town to Point Loma.

Derby explained that whichever plan the Corps selected, the riverbed's grainy, quicksand-like substratum required driving piles deep into the bed to stabilize the structure. The engineer noted that the slopes of the mesa near Presidio Hill contained an abundance of gravel, soil and stones suitable for construction materials. In the context of an 1850s construction project in a remote location, the specifics of Derby's plan speak to the rudimentary engineering aspects of the project and the equipment and technical assistance at his disposal. This was a simple project to be performed with manual labor and basic equipment.

Derby dispatched his findings, map and proposals to Chief of Engineers Abert in March 1853. The budget-conscious board of engineers inevitably settled for the least expensive concept, essentially a bulkhead and a ditch.

The *San Diego Herald* presciently chided the government's decision to ignore Derby's more extensive plan, but with Congress handling the purse strings for a project in a tiny town three thousand miles from Washington, D.C., the federal government appeared not so much improvident as simply frugal. President Franklin Pierce nearly canceled Derby's project when the fiscally conservative chief executive vetoed, and Congress sustained, the Rivers and Harbors legislation that funded the project. Derby beseeched his superiors to appropriate funds from the army's discretionary funds. His superiors initially refused the request but eventually relented and allowed Derby to move forward but with the construction of an even less substantial bulkhead. Frustrated with government's apparent lack of purpose, the engineer requested a transfer, which his superiors summarily denied.

Derby opened construction in July 1853. In an attempt to make the project both economical and expeditious, and worried that he could not complete the job before the onset of the rainy season, Derby eschewed the normal government bidding and contract process. He purchased $200 worth of supplies from Philip Crosthwaite's mercantile store in Old Town; gathered carts, shovels and wheelbarrows; hired laborers; and set the men to work. Derby mustered a labor force that included local white men and American Indians from neighboring ranches. Years later, the *San Diego Union* reported that the construction began with around thirty white men working under two American overseers and forty-seven mission Indians working under the supervision of their own chiefs, Manuelito of the Luisenos and Old Tomas of the Kumeyaays. Derby paid the white laborers between $50 and $60 per month, but there is no record of the pay scale for the Indians. Apparently at least one African American man worked on the job. According to Derby's racial-laced account in the *Herald*, the tenure of this "purson" was a short-lived experience that ended after a lunchtime altercation. According to the news item, at the midday break of his first workday, other laborers, "mostly from southern states," objected when a man of "colored persuasion" sat down at their table. When the overseer "civilly" informed the African American laborer that the cook would prepare a separate repast for him, the man "stated publically that he cared not a d--n for the entire crowd" and noted that if he "was not able to eat with them he was not able to work in their society" and walked off the job.[4]

Apparently, on days when he wanted to avoid the long walk across the sandy river flats, Derby watched the levee work from his second-story bedroom window in the Pendleton House. Whether it was a time or budget concern, Derby ordered the workers to deepen the existing, twisted channel rather than creating the new straight trench he originally envisioned. Following the government's recommendations, and against his better judgment to build a more substantial structure, Derby constructed the levee base with loose soil faced with rock on a sandy ridge, with slopes falling away from the levee's crest in both directions. That decision proved fatal. As Derby predicted and the Coastal Survey of 1858 confirmed, the levee as constructed was in reality a temporary structure. The high water events over the next two years inexorably eroded the levee and left it in a dilapidated state, and the major flood of 1861–62 swept away the weakened levee. By 1862, the river was again pouring into the harbor. And what became of Derby? Unfortunately and perhaps unfairly, he became better known in San Diego for his literary talents than his engineering skills.

The failure of the levee renewed the town's subsequent efforts to reconnect with the government and build another structure. Most San Diego boosters believed that with a new levee, the resurrected harbor would fulfill the town's quest for maritime expansion.

The Levee of 1876

With the Derby Dike in shambles, the San Diego River once again flowed uncontested into the harbor, and the optimism of San Diego citizens faded along with the government's interest in revitalizing the project. An editorial in the December 1868 *San Diego Union* complained that rather than trying to rectify the situation, the desultory efforts of Congress resulted "in nothing more demonstrative than expensive opinions of impracticable scribblers, and surveys and specifications of gigantic paper wasters and indefatable [sic] ciphers."[5] Whether it was legislative pressure or national self-interest, certainly not the wrath of the *Union*, sixteen years after the Derby levee disappeared, the government responded.

In May 1869, Secretary of War General John A. Rawlins ordered Chief of Engineers General Andrew A. Humphreys to send an engineer to San Diego to conduct a new comprehensive harbor survey and recommend measures for turning the river back into False Bay. The promising start almost generated the opposite result when Humphreys assigned Major Robert S. Williamson, the commander of the San Francisco District, to conduct the survey. The major had an unsettled history with the citizens of San Diego.

In the 1850s, Williamson headed a topographical survey to determine the best routes for a transcontinental railway. In his final report, Williamson categorized the San Diego route as impractical and endorsed the passage that favored San Diego's municipal nemesis, Los Angeles. Then Williamson recommended the government expend a sizeable amount in Wilmington rather than on San Diego Harbor. The perceived favoritism made the engineer an unpopular figure in San Diego.

San Diegans expressed some relief when Williamson delegated the survey to a subordinate, Lieutenant William H. Heuer. Heuer arrived in October 1869 with an assignment to ascertain if the San Diego River had formed any new sand flats at or near the river's mouth or on either side of the harbor's channel and then report if the river's encroachment had seriously endangered the harbor. Heuer quickly confirmed that the most significant changes in the harbor had occurred in the flats near Old Town, where the San Diego River encroached into the bay. The engineer observed that the flat near the channel running into the bay had increased almost three hundred feet in width, and on the west side of the bay, the channel had narrowed over two hundred feet and was twenty feet shallower. Paradoxically, Heuer offered the opinion that in terms of commerce, the harbor was as good as it was in 1856 and concluded that the river's detritus had not adversely affected the harbor over the last fourteen years. Heuer also recognized that much of the old sand flat the Derby levee crossed was now privately owned and feared the possibility of protracted lawsuits. Then he proposed placing a four-thousand-foot-long dam or bulkhead across the mouth of Mission Valley. Heuer forwarded his final situational assessment to Williamson in San Francisco, which Williamson followed with his assessment sent to Chief of Engineers Humphreys in December 1869. In his report, Williamson stated that because there was only a comparatively slight change in depth over the entry bar since 1856, which he believed did not impair the value of the harbor, he felt that a new levee project was unnecessary. The action left San Diegans both confused and optimistic.

COL WM. H. Heuer
Aug 31, 1905 - Oct 16, 1905

Lieutenant William H. Heuer conducted preliminary surveys for the new levee in the early 1870s. *Los Angeles District, U.S. Army Corps of Engineers.*

While the government debated and San Diegans worried, in 1870 a group of San Diego businessmen organized the San Diego Chamber of Commerce. The chamber's professed purpose was to promote the city's interests and advocate for civic development. Cognizant of the importance of the harbor in growing the city, and perhaps reacting to the memories of recent flood events, the chamber members immediately formed a Harbor Committee and set out to revitalize the levee project. The committee members enlisted the service of California congressman Sherman O. Houghton to champion their cause. Unfortunately, reality stifled expectation, and the pleas of Congressman Houghton and the chamber fell on unresponsive legislative ears.

The chamber directors renewed their efforts to reopen the project after a severe winter rainstorm unleashed a sediment-saturated torrent into the upper bay. The committee dispatched telegrams to California senator Aaron A. Sargent and Congressman Houghton that urged the legislators to use their influence to gain an appropriation to protect the harbor. In this campaign, the chamber directors attempted to assuage the image that local self-interest drove the levee project. They reiterated the professional opinions of past government surveys that touted the excellence of San Diego Bay and fixed the onus on the government to address a new levee project and protect a valuable national asset.[6]

Rhetoric aside, the officers of the Pacific Division of the Army Corps of Engineers were acutely aware of the harbor's degradation. When Lieutenant John H. Weeden of the Corps, already in San Diego working on the fortifications at Fort Rosecrans, rendered his impressions of the harbor situation to Los Angeles district supervisor General B.S. Alexander in April 1871, the Pacific Division officials reacted. General Alexander dispatched Lieutenant Thomas H. Handbury to San Diego in January 1872 to formally investigate. Handbury reported back to Alexander that, in his estimation, if the river was not redirected it would eventually fill and ruin San Diego Harbor.

At the federal government level, Houghton informed the chamber membership that he had inserted an item into a pending bill that requested another survey of the harbor. The bill passed in June 1872, and the chairman of the Committee on Appropriations reassured Houghton that Congress would undoubtedly approve the San Diego levee project in the subsequent session. Then, in mid-1874, acting on the recommendation of Corps of Engineers Major George H. Mendell, who believed that the consequences of the river's encroachment were important enough to warrant federal action, Secretary of War William W. Belknap persuaded the Senate to take action. The senators passed an appropriation in June 1874, with a narrow 23–20 vote, that included funding for the river project. In March 1875, a Congressional River and Harbors Act formally approved $80,000 to construct a new levee.

With the Congressional appropriation authorized, Lieutenant Colonel C. Seaforth Stewart of the Corps directed Lieutenant Weeden back to San Diego for a new survey. Weeden collected pertinent data, generated a map with the project's parameters and presented those findings to Stewart in June 1876. Working from Weeden's data, Stewart and the Corps engineers recommended a 7,700-foot embankment that extended across the river's alluvial path from the high ground near Old Town westward to Point Loma, with a berm excavated along the front of the structure for extra protection. To strengthen and stabilize the structure, the plan recommended covering the face of the levee with broken stone, or riprap; excavating a new canal for the river channel; and, to protect the crest, planting willow, eucalyptus trees and brush on the upper surface. Stewart also suggested a strong fence to surround the completed structure to prevent the encroachment of cattle, sheep and horses, which he was told wandered the sand flats and foraged in the area during dry weather.

Using this data, in early September 1875, Stewart presented Humphreys with four construction scenarios that varied in cost from $75,000 to $158,000. Significantly, Stewart did not include the cost of land. With the proposals near or over the allotted $80,000, Stewart recommended that his Washington minders refer the project profiles to the Corps regional office in San Francisco for discussion and final approval.

The Pacific Coast Board of Engineers tasked to review the project consisted of Mendell, Stewart and Board President Lieutenant Colonel Alexander. The three-man committee studied the problem, weighed the alternatives and arrived at different conclusions. Stewart and Alexander suggested an earthen embankment extending from below Presidio Hill in Old Town westward to Point Loma. Their plan called for a 6-foot-high embankment with a 23-foot crest, faced with riprap of broken stone that rested on a footwall of dry stone. The cost for this earthen dike came in at the exact appropriation amount of $80,000. Mendell, the Corps jetty expert, accepted the levee concept but believed that the addition of a series of twenty-five stone jetties protruding into the channel every 250 to 300 feet would strengthen and protect the structure. Mendell reasoned that jetties would divert the waters away from the structure and render it less vulnerable to undermining.[7]

Jetty expert George Mendel recommended a series of small jetties along the face of the new levee. *Los Angeles District, U.S. Army Corps of Engineers.*

Secretary Belknap considered the options and then approved the majority plan on November 5, 1875. But with the Southern California rainy season approaching, the on-site engineers deferred the start of the project until the spring of 1876.

The Pacific Board released the project to bid in mid-March 1876 and received and reviewed thirteen contractor responses. The board seriously considered ten of the bids, five from San Francisco and five from San Diego, before awarding Johnson and Schuyler of San Diego the contract with a bid of $79,798.72. Captain George A. Johnson was the first customs collector for the Port of San Diego and owner of the Los Penasquitos Rancho north of San Diego. Howard Schuyler was a local contractor with business ties to San Francisco. The board scheduled the work to begin on May 15, 1876, but when the contractors alerted the board that the government did not have title to all the requisite lands, the Corps engineers postponed the starting date indefinitely.

As Heuer predicted in 1869, the government's failure to acquire the land the levee bisected became a major obstacle. Stewart had mistakenly reasoned that because the city had shown no previous interest in purchasing the sites, the land in question held little or no value. In an attempt to preempt the issue, Colonel Stewart directed Weeden to meet and negotiate with the landowners. Confused ownership claims, the number of claimants, disputed land titles (several holdings were under the names of deceased persons) and the fact that more than a few disgruntled lot owners were ready to sue the government exacerbated the already muddled situation and created a logistical nightmare for Weeden.

The price for the now desirable land was the impasse. The government valued the Pueblo Lots on the sand flat from $5 to $10 per acre and the more desirable lots near Old Town at $60. The owners countered with values at $20 to $50 and $400 to $600, respectively. As the negotiations lurched forward and the owners maintained their demand for what Stewart considered exorbitant prices, condemning the land appeared the government's only resort.

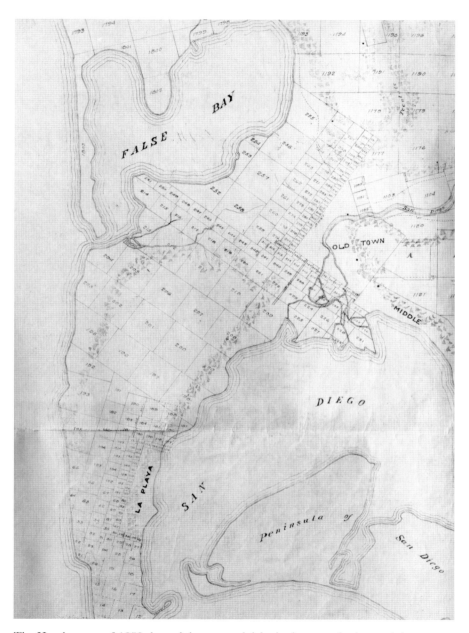

The Hensley map of 1873 showed the renewed delta in the upper harbor and the privately owned lots on the sandy flat that a new levee would cross. *San Diego Public Library Map Collection.*

Reluctantly, Stewart opened condemnation proceedings through the California State Attorney General's Office in Sacramento. According to California law, one hundred days must pass before condemnation proceeding became actionable. In March, the State Assembly passed a bill to convey the designated real estate to the government, and a California State panel determined the total value on the condemned land at $1,600. On May 13, the mediators filed their report, and on the twenty-ninth, the government paid the claimants $1,524 in open court and took title to the properties.

On June 5, 1876, Weeden released contractors Johnson and Schuyler to commence work. The contractors started at the opposite ends of the levee and worked inward. By the end of the month, workers on the west terminus had excavated the channel to half its average depth and constructed the corresponding portion of the levee, while the men at the Old Town tip had built and faced about 350 feet of the levee. The clay-laden soil the workers quarried from the slopes near Presidio Hill proved so stable that the contractors reduced the height of the first 2,300 feet of the eastern end of the levee. The builders faced the front slope of the levee and the trench beneath the slope with smooth, hard cobblestone gathered from the slopes adjacent to Old Town.

The project progressed smoothly until the contractors brought in thirty Chinese laborers from San Francisco. The contractors hoped to accelerate the construction with the extra labor and assigned the experienced men the masonry work. The white laborers immediately stopped work, organized mass meetings to discuss the "Chinese cheap labor" question and selected a committee to meet with Johnson and discuss the situation. Johnson quickly announced that the Chinese men would only work at jobs the white laborers were unwilling to perform. He also assured the white workers that he had already promised work to thirty or forty more white men and believed that the project would generate work for "all the laboring men in San Diego who wanted it."[8] Mollified, the white and Chinese laborers set to work, although as segregated groups.

The citizens of San Diego celebrated the American centennial with fireworks, speeches and the knowledge that their levee was well underway. The levee project was the biggest show in town. Local kibitzers gathered at the construction site to watch the progress with both interest and wariness, while local newspapers presented a running commentary on the construction. The opening salvo of construction was just that: a prodigious explosion resulted when Captain Johnson planted forty kegs of powder near Presidio Hill to blast out some earth and stone for the project. Local

This view of the levee in the late 1890s looked east up Mission Valley. *Los Angeles District, U.S. Army Corps of Engineers.*

legend held that the explosion indeed loosened a mass of earth and rock but also destroyed what remained of the original adobe walls of the old presidio. Progress had its consequences.

By September, the project had taken on a steady rhythm. The *Union* reported that there were about fifty teams at work on the embankment, including seventy-five Chinese workers, with about an equal number of white laborers. Johnson and the subcontractors paid $5,000 per month for labor, with $1,500 going to the Chinese workers and the balance to the white labor force. The working conditions proved perfect, and the levee rapidly took form. Four months into the job, the embankment reached 3,400 feet in length from Presidio Hill, with the workers extending the structure an average of 500 feet per week. With a 15-foot-wide crest, a 40-foot base and standing 5 feet high, the structure was both shorter and narrower than specified in the original designs. The job supervisors assigned the Chinese laborers the task of facing the levee with stone quarried from the Presidio and Stockton hills. The *Union* characterized the stonework of the Chinese workers as very precise and described the finished wall as "exceedingly handsome" and built in a substantial and durable manner.[9]

If Weeden and his associates lacked Derby's colorful personality, their collective skills certainly proved worthy to the task. The Corps supervisors announced the project completed on November 6, 1876, two months ahead of schedule. Weeden conducted his final inspection and pronounced that Johnson and Schuyler performed the work in a thoroughly satisfactory and workmanlike manner; then he noted that because the contractors had used extra stone, no money remained to fence the perimeter of the levee.

With the contract fulfilled, Stewart reported the final numbers for the project. The levee was officially 7,734.64 feet in length and had consumed $79,789.72 of the $80,000 appropriation. Facts were fine, but what really mattered to the people of San Diego were Stewart's words lauding the levee as a structure that would preserve their harbor and benefit regional commerce.

San Diegans applauded the result, but their rivals in Los Angeles, of course, offered a more cynical view. The *Los Angeles Times* decried the $80,000 Congressional appropriation for the levee as an "outrage" and suggested that the government could have put the money to better use on

The 7,700-foot-long levee completed in 1876 permanently stemmed the river, protected the harbor and renewed the town's maritime aspirations. *Los Angeles District, U.S. Army Corps of Engineers.*

The levee as it appeared in 1914 topped with a roadway and utility poles. *San Diego History Center.*

the harbor project in Los Angeles. The *Union* jabbed back and reminded its rival that Wilmington would need every penny of the $500,000 appropriation to improve its so-called harbor.[10] Insults aside, San Diego had its levee, and the harbor was secure.

Floods over the next three decades necessitated some repairs, but well into the 1930s, the levee remained sound and protected the harbor from the river. The project also convinced San Diego business leaders that they could successfully lobby Congress for continued harbor improvements and hopefully lure the U.S. Navy to San Diego. Obliquely, San Diego's military future was the legacy of Derby's failed venture.

Today, the levee exists as a sloping rock embankment on the southern edge of the San Diego River Floodway that parallels Interstate 8 and extends from Presidio Park to the mouth of the river at Dog Beach in Ocean Beach. The Estuary Trail, a 3.75-mile-long segment of the San Diego River Trail, runs along the levee's crest. The only reminder of the old levee is Levee Street, a short dead-end paved road that runs beside the Estuary Trail and passes in front of the Peninsula Tennis Club in the Robb Field Recreation area.

Chapter 4

THE SAN DIEGO FLUME COMPANY
DEVELOPS THE RIVER

Water on our coastal lands is surely the blood of the soil.
—Ed Fletcher, San Diego water entrepreneur and manager
of the Cuyamaca Water Company

The first truly notable enterprise on the river in the American years was Theodore S. Van Dyke's formation of the San Diego Flume Company in 1886. With the realization that water development was the key to San Diego's future, Van Dyke envisioned a large-scale private water company as the path to entrepreneurial success. Also, given the town's current water distress, he believed that the timing seemed perfect for such a venture. San Diego's William Smythe, a contemporary of Van Dyke's, described Flume's slightly built, bearded founder as a Renaissance man, skilled as an author, hunter, engineer, farmer and lawyer. Smythe should have included dreamer and visionary.

In the mid-1880s, Van Dyke and fellow water promoter William E. Robinson conceived the idea of bringing river water out of the Cuyamaca Mountains to San Diego's sixteen thousand downstream domestic and irrigation users. In late 1885, the pair named their original scheme the San Diego Irrigation Company and dispatched engineers into the upper reaches of the river to survey and confirm the plausibility of the venture. Satisfied with their findings, Van Dyke filed a water claim in what he called the "San Diego River canyon." Van Dyke's scheme centered on the construction of a system of wooden troughs, trestles and aqueducts to

Left: Theodore Van Dyke designed the San Diego Flume system to bring water out of the interior mountains to San Diego consumers. *Helix Water District.*

Below: The redwood flume gravity-flowed water over thirty miles to San Diego. *Lakeside Historical Society.*

deliver an annual water supply out of the mountains over thirty miles to downstream consumers, specifically the citizens of San Diego.[1] Van Dyke realized his ambition in 1886 when he gathered investors and formed the San Diego Flume Company.

Van Dyke surveyed and mapped out a route and then hired the Sacramento contractors Carle, Croly & Abernathy to construct the conveyance system. The system started at a small masonry diversion dam on the river just below the mouth of Boulder Creek, a westward-flowing tributary of the San Diego River. The dam collected water from the river and water from an alpine storage reservoir, Lake Cuyamaca, situated at the headwaters of Boulder Creek, and fed the water into the delivery system. The redwood chute, the flume, generally paralleled the river as it ran southward from the small dam. With periodic release points along the route, the wooden trough cut across mountainsides, passed through tunnels with masonry walls and timber ceilings and crossed over towering wooden trestles before the flume terminated at collection points at the small Eucalyptus and Grossmont Reservoirs. From these reservoirs, located about ten miles outside San Diego, Flume operators released water into an earthen conduit, which transported the water into a three-thousand-foot-long redwood stave pipe that emptied into the La Mesa Ditch and ultimately into the La Mesa Reservoir. A steel pipeline moved the water from the La Mesa Reservoir to the city distributing system at University Heights. It is noteworthy that while the flume followed the river through the El Capitan Grande Indian Reservation, Van Dyke started construction without the approval of the Department of the Interior, which supervised the federal land the flume crossed, or permission from the Capitan Grande people living on the reservation.

The scope and potential of the project captured the imagination of the citizens of water-starved San Diego. In July 1886, the *San Diego Union* detailed Van Dyke's grand undertaking and heralded the new water venture as "the greatest enterprise yet undertaken in San Diego County."[2] The willing public accepted Van Dyke's estimation that the system would deliver six thousand miner's inches of water (an engineering term to describe a unit of water flow, about 11.22 gallons per minute) to the town and sixty thousand inches to ranchers. Most San Diegans viewed the completion of Van Dyke's Flume as a seminal engineering event that offered the city an opportunity to achieve water sustainability. Unfortunately, the first prolonged dry spell revealed the system's faults.

The Flume opened operations in February 1889 to citywide celebrations. The festivities culminated with local and state dignitaries floating down the

Construction of the wooden trough required more than 9 million board feet of imported redwood and two years of labor. *From William H. Hall's 1888 State Report.*

The thirty-four-foot-high masonry diverting dam created a reservoir that regulated the water flow into the Flume system. *City of San Diego Water Department Archive.*

completed trough in small boats. The fact that the water in the Flume that day was piped in from the San Diego Water Company system did little to dampen the public jubilation. The first water from the system's diverting dam arrived downstream some three weeks later.

San Diego banker Joseph W. Sefton financed the engineering feat that Van Dyke designed, and Van Dyke's friend William Robinson served as the first general manager. It was a costly venture. According to the data from the Helix Water District, building Cuyamaca Dam cost $54,000; the diverting dam, which required additional repairs, cost $50,000; and the six-foot-wide-by-sixteen-inch-deep wooden trough, which required 9 million board feet of two-inch redwood to construct, cost approximately $700,000. State Engineer Hammond Hall estimated that the owners expended approximately $1 million to put the flume in operation. The system produced the longest wooden flume in the world; included more than 315 trestles, with Los Coches Trestle the highest at 65 feet and longest at 1,774 feet; and passed through eight tunnels on its 33.21-mile journey. Van Dyke and his associates considered the Flume Company a long-term, for-profit business undertaking and realized that negotiating a contract with the city, the region's largest consumer, was vital to their success.

Ambition and the engineering accomplishment aside, the Flume experienced a timorous beginning. In retrospect, Van Dyke opined that internal mismanagement and, in his opinion, the "stupidity of the board of directors" negatively affected the company's progress. He believed that the directors were more interested in personal matters and land speculation

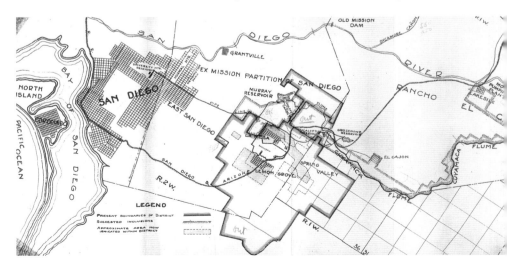

than overseeing the development and well-being of the company.[3] In the opinion of San Diego historian William Smythe, the backcountry real estate speculators on the company's board were so engrossed in their own schemes that they ignored the enterprise. Van Dyke commented that as he and his compatriots struggled to extract water out of the mountains, naysayers maintained that the Flume managers were "mere fools monkeying" around with an impracticable scheme of no consequence.[4] Twice in 1895 a frustrated Van Dyke attempted to sell the enterprise to the city—in February for $900,000 and then in July for $1.5 million. Van Dyke's dream had become an insolvent, burdensome, unreliable business endeavor.

For all its promise, the San Diego Flume was a flawed system. The distance the water traveled; the flume's inadequate construction, which required constant repairs; and the system's reliability on a small watershed that depended on unpredictable seasonal runoff plagued the venture from the start. The system also experienced an unanticipated and troublesome problem with the amount of debris that clogged the flume chute. Once workers cleared the wooden channel of tree branches, leaves and dead animals, young adventurers, and sometimes drunken miners, enjoyed late-night float trips, which often damaged the trough and generally irritated the farmers along the line. In the low water months, the slow-moving water that flowed for miles over leaky, rough-hewn planks was susceptible to evaporation

The flume conveyed water from the diverting dam to the downstream storage reservoirs and then to the town's distribution system. *Helix Water District.*

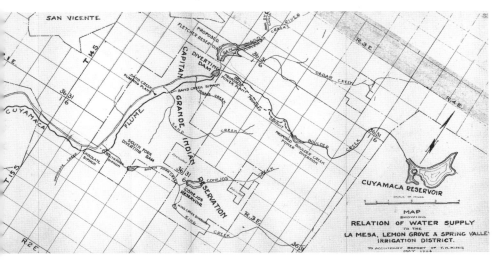

The flume tunneled through hillsides and crossed over canyons via hundreds of wooden trestles. *Lakeside Historical Society.*

The aging wooden flume required engineers to constantly conduct inspections and dispatch work crews to make repairs. *Helix Water District.*

and of questionable quality. Flume officials promised an abundance of water of the best quality; unfortunately, the system more often delivered less water than needed and too often water unfit for household use.

The collapse of the regional land boom in the late 1880s; a succession of below-average rainy seasons, which depleted the system's water supply and left the river water brackish and undrinkable; lingering financial difficulties; and recurring construction issues rendered the Flume Company a struggling enterprise. Public confidence in the system also dimmed. The *San Diego Union* reflected public sentiment when the paper editorialized that even under the "most favorable circumstances," most people believed that the system did not have the capacity to store enough water to service the community from one season to the next.[5] When the drought of 1897–1900 eroded the system's delivery efficiency, Van Dyke sold the company to M.C. Healion and a group of the Flume's British bondholders. Van Dyke's and San Diego's first true water venture had faltered within a decade. Like Van Dyke, the new owners hoped to commercialize the system through the sale of water to the city and supplying irrigation water to the interior valleys, but the 1905 drought and legal woes again drove the company further into financial distress.

The company had tittered on the edge of credibility and fiduciary stability as natural, administrative and technical complexities simply overwhelmed successive owners. For all the Flume's shortcomings, its presence advertised the region, and its tacit promise of a steady water supply lured new settlers to San Diego. The Flume Company remained the county's most ambitious major private water venture until John D. Spreckels gained control of Otay Water Company and formed the Southern California Mountain Water Company (SCMWC) in 1905. Spreckels's political clout undoubtedly influenced Mayor John Sehon to approve a city ordinance that year that allowed the city to accept a rate that essentially ordained the Flume Company's demise.

After years of insolvency, the British consortium admitted that the Flume Company was a failed venture. Enter local water entrepreneur and opportunist Ed Fletcher. Almost prophetically, Fletcher had arrived with his parents in San Diego from Massachusetts the same year the county's greatest water venture started operations. He applied his emerging talents to develop water and real estate schemes with the understanding that water brought value to the land. Fletcher was an adept salesman with a particular ability to share his entrepreneurial visions with others, particularly those of means. A contemporary described the six-foot-tall, clean-shaven Fletcher as an energetic man with a classic profile and high, broad forehead capped with dark, wavy hair, and he was in possession of an open, friendly personality that made him a persuasive communicator, a talent Fletcher used to his advantage throughout his business and political career.

Fate intervened in 1910 when a third party introduced Fletcher to wealthy Montana businessman James Murray. Murray amassed his fortune after striking it rich in Montana and then investing in mining, banking, real estate and regional waterworks. Murray believed that San Diego was an inviting market for investment and sought a person familiar with the area to act as his representative. Murray thought that Fletcher was the perfect fit.

Apparently, Fletcher convinced Murray that the faltering Flume was an undervalued enterprise and partnered with him to purchase the company for $150,000. By the articles of incorporation issued in July 1913, Murray held five thousand shares and Fletcher one thousand, a one-sixth interest, with each share valued at $100. Fletcher had managed his own small water company for a decade, but joining with Murray as a minor partner was his first foray into a water venture with countywide implications. Murray left no doubt about who controlled the business—he was the financier and decision-maker and tasked Fletcher with applying his energetic managing skills to daily operations, securing contracts and increasing revenues.[6] Fletcher approached the new business venture and the impending relationship between the company and the city in light of the old western water management aphorism that suggested it was better to be upstream with a shovel and a ditch than downstream with a decree.

The new Flume owners renamed the company the Cuyamaca Water Company (CWC). As successful businessmen, Fletcher and Murray fully expected to transform the struggling, unstable company into a profitable undertaking. The old Flume Company's assets were considerable, but at the time of acquisition, the Flume was a twenty-two-year-old system in a state of physical and financial decline and with a tarnished reputation as a water supplier. Murray and Fletcher accepted that the CWC was a risky investment but believed that they were uniquely qualified to overcome the organization's deficiencies and make it a profitable enterprise.

Following the purchase, Murray requested William Post, the company's chief engineer, to conduct a survey to determine the condition of the system. Post's report concluded that the system had substantial deficiencies. The shallow, decaying redwood conveyance trough was susceptible to leaks and evaporation when functioning and became warped, cracked and uneven when the water stopped running. Post noted that the system's limited catchment and single small reservoir would seriously curtail water availability in times of drought, that the system's storage apparatus was inadequate and that the dam was not configured to capture floodwater but rather was only a small diversion unit with a limited capacity. In Post's judgment, the Flume operators faced the dilemma of trying to meet customer demands with less water than their system could supply.

The owners premised the future of the company on improving the system and making their enterprise a major water provider to San Diego. As they struggled to stabilize the company in 1912, the CWC became entangled in a newspaper war with John Spreckels and his SCMWC over which water agency would be the principal municipal provider. The Spreckels backers painted Fletcher and Murray as profit-minded opportunists and portrayed

In 1910, James A. Murray, a wealthy Montana businessman, partnered with Ed Fletcher, purchased the San Diego Flume Company and renamed it the Cuyamaca Water Company. *From Ed Fletcher's* Memoirs.

Spreckels as a public-minded citizen who promised to apply the earning from his water sale to construct an eastern railroad route into the city. The Spreckels-owned *San Diego Union* labeled those who opposed the sale of his water company to the city "Socialists." Supporters of the CWC struck back in kind through the friendly *San Diego Sun*, where Fletcher harped that Spreckels's social and civic status allowed him to exert intense public pressure that unduly influenced the Common Council to purchase the SCMWC rather than the CWC. In February 1913, the city purchased the SCMWC.

Fletcher shrugged off the feud with Spreckels and continued to upgrade the CWC to make it attractive to any potential buyer. Fletcher and Post formulated an improvement plan that included performing routine maintenance, placing new groundwater pumping stations on the riverbed, repairing the wooden flume, constructing additional water storage facilities and building as many as five new dams and associated reservoirs on the tributaries that fed the San Diego River. The most significant system enhancement occurred when Fletcher convinced Murray to finance the construction of a new dam to replace the old La Mesa Dam and increase the storage capacity at the Flume's terminus. (After Murray's death in 1921,

Fletcher renamed the new 117-foot-high multi-arch in Murray's honor.) Fletcher also ordered the pumps at the river groundwater station in El Monte rebuilt and electrified. In spite of Fletcher's efforts, the company's uneven business and the expense of implementing upgrades changed the owners' strategy from improving the system to increase efficiency to making the system more attractive to potential buyers.

City water bureaucrats watched the evolution of the CWC with suspicion and unease. City leaders gladly purchased water from the CWC—that was business—but they would not tolerate the CWC encroaching on their control over the waters of the river. In successive city resolutions, policy-makers emphasized that any agreement that the city made with the CWC was not a precedent or an indication that the city abdicated any right to the river's waters. The city's stance was clear: the river belonged to the city, and the CWC could not encroach on that right.

Besides conflict with the city and Spreckels, the CWC managers also encountered issues with local riparian water owners. Fletcher's real estate ties to the east county and his tactic of using domestic water as the CWC's principal profit stream alienated many back county consumers. In 1913, ranchers in the El Cajon Valley secured a temporary injunction to prevent

To increase the system's capacity, in 1918 the company owners constructed a controversial multiple-arch storage dam, later renamed Murray Dam. *San Diego City Water Department Archive.*

the CWC from pumping San Diego River groundwater, their principal irrigation source, for city domestic use. Fletcher responded to the injunction with the argument that such a prohibition would place a hardship on his company and its fifteen to twenty thousand consumers during the current water famine. Over the next several years, CWC representatives appeared before the California State Railroad Commission, the state's water regulatory agency since 1911, on fifteen occasions to hear complaints against the CWC's rates and mode of operation.

Fletcher also contended with a mandate from the State Railway Commission to reline the leaky flume chute. The commissioners recommended a concrete surfacing, but the cost-conscious Flume manager had other ideas. One local recollection said that Fletcher ordered workers to resurface the trough with tarpaper tacked down with roofing nails and then sealed with a tar-slurry. Apparently Fletcher paid local contractor Roscoe Hazard $44,000 to reline the flume with a rubberized roofing material. Fletcher boasted to the California State Railroad Commissioners that the relining was a "howling success," but his doubters were much less sanguine. A California State Engineering Report in March 1925 declared the system in a dilapidated and highly precarious condition.[7]

After managing the system for fifteen years, Murray and Fletcher admitted that the company was failing. In his correspondence, Fletcher complained that the enterprise was "never a paying investment" and that managing the company had caused him "more anguish and worry" and generated "less profit than any other venture in my life's experience." He often referred to the CWC as a "headache." In a letter to his lawyer friend Walter Huber, Fletcher characterized the company as a "losing game" that "never paid a dividend" and that was being "bled to death" by litigation.[8] In a letter to Councilman Fred Heilbron in April 1919, Fletcher admitted that Murray barely paid the company's operating expenses, and after expending approximately $1 million on the system, they had not received a dollar in dividends.[9]

By 1920, Murray and Fletcher were fixated on selling the company to the city. From a purely business standpoint, the physical state of the flume system and its questionable profitability explained their persistent efforts to sell the system. Fletcher offered the CWC to the city in 1913 for approximately $300,000; in 1917 for $746,000; in 1922, after Murray's death, for $1 million; and in 1925 for $1.5 million. The amounts and dates varied according to different contemporary sources, but the owners' desire to divest the business never wavered. On each occasion, city leaders deflected the overtures and maintained their stance over the city's control of the river. Fletcher understood that the indifference of city leaders stemmed from their strategy to maintain leverage over the rights to the river. He also accepted that the majority of the Common Council believed that the Cuyamaca system was simply old and overvalued.

But Fletcher also believed that in addition to political differences, there was also a portion of personal animus involved. Fletcher was specifically convinced that the deep-seated rivalry he experienced with John Spreckels had motivated the town's wealthiest man to use his considerable business and political influence to block the sale of the CWC to the city. In Fletcher's view, there were individuals in city government aligned against him. During his testimony at the 1918 Congressional hearings, Fletcher stated that he was "not accusing anybody or any councilman being in the pay of any man, but it is that influence behind the Council, that in my opinion keeps us from selling the Cuyamaca Water system to the city."[10] According to historian William Wright, it appeared that the majority of the members of the Common Council, the lead agency in city water matters, did not approach the sales offers with any "trustful enthusiasm." Wright speculated that both the council members and Fletcher worried that one party was always trying to "put one over" on the other.[11] Fletcher's fears were not unfounded. During a meeting between the members of the Common Council and the City Water Commission in January 1921, when City Water Commissioner Charles Chandler asked where the city stood with Fletcher, fellow member Julius Wangeheim answered, "We don't stand at all, the Fletcher interests are merely trying to block every move the city makes." Councilman Steward added that any efforts by Fletcher to divert the waters of the San Diego River should be met with an injunction. In 1921, the Common Council issued a statement declaring that the city would "fight to the limit" any action from individuals or organizations that interfered with the municipality's rights to the river. The atmosphere of mutual distrust made general negotiations difficult and sales proposals improbable and set the tone for future encounters.

The specter of years of expensive litigation coupled with the futile attempts to sell the CWC compelled Fletcher to offer the company to the La Mesa, Lemon Grove and Spring Valley Irrigation District in 1924. Instead of providing a solution to the problem, the offer exacerbated the tension between the CWC and the city. Officials in city hall perceived Fletcher's sales overture to the irrigation district as a strategy to pressure the city into purchasing the CWC. In part, Fletcher's idea worked. The sales proposal prompted a meeting between Fletcher and City Councilman Fred Heilbron. In the course of the negotiations between the longtime friends, Fletcher offered the dam sites at El Capitan and Mission Gorge no. 3, Murray Dam and other distribution lines in the CWC system to the city to enhance the sales offer. In turn, Fletcher asked for the city's approval to build his new dam on the upper river and a guaranteed division of river water. The men appeared to seek common ground but failed to reach an agreement. Again city officials balked to take any action that Fletcher might construe as a precedent concerning the river, and again the council refused to grant the CWC any river water it perceived the city already owned. The California State Supreme Court finally approved the sale of the CWC to the irrigation district in January 1926 for $1.4 million. The irrigation district became a public water agency, which placed Fletcher, at least in appearance, on the periphery of litigation that now engaged two local governments.

The CWC and its successor, the La Mesa, Lemon Grove and Spring Valley Irrigation District, physically exerted a minimal influence on the river. The company captured a small amount of the river flow almost thirty miles upstream. When the dry season reduced the river to base flow levels, the Flume took a more significant portion of the river water, but during the rainy season, the amount was inconsequential compared to the river's flow. Nor did the diversions into the Flume system significantly change the hydrology of the river. The operations of the Flume Company and the CWC left the middle and lower sections of the river largely unaffected. But philosophically, at least to city water advocates and the Common Council, the systems posed a potential threat to the city's claim to the river. Civic bureaucrats viewed regional water development as an essential stimulus to municipal growth, and the exclusive control of the San Diego River, the county's largest water resource, was the key. Spreckels's son Claus perhaps explained the situation best when he stated that there could only be one master of the river. The scene was set for years of bitter litigation.

Chapter 5

EARLY RIVER MISADVENTURES

Among the enterprises of genuine merit…a foremost place must be given to the Junipero Land and Water Company.
—San Diego Union, *February 1888*

The San Diego Flume Company was not the only private water enterprise that organized to commercialize the waters of the San Diego River. The years following San Diego's frenzied real estate boom of the mid-1880s spawned a plethora of private entrepreneurial land and water ventures. Countywide promotions included the Mount Tecarte Land and Water Company, the San Felipe Land and Water Company, the Santa Maria Land and Water Company and the Teralta Land and Water Company. These promoters launched elaborate speculative schemes to place water on the sparsely populated lands surrounding the town and cultivated the vision of transforming the parched lands of San Diego into vernal freshness. These profit-oriented organizers hoped—for personal, professional and civic reasons—to boost the local economy and spur municipal growth. Most of these venture capitalists found that in semi-arid San Diego, water was a commodity that was easy to promise and promote but difficult to develop and deliver. All of these speculative schemes were ambitious, some even audacious, but most failed.

Irrigation districts had sprouted across California following the California state legislature's enactment of the Wright Act of 1887. The act provided for the organization and management of irrigation districts, granted them powers of eminent domain and taxation and allowed small farmers to band together to pool resources. In San Diego, the economic value of water on land and the possibility of combining agricultural and urban water needs tantalized business opportunists. And the time was right. At the end of the 1880s, land prices dropped faster and further than they had risen, and San Diego's speculative real estate boom collapsed from the developing economic depress, the ongoing drought and its own inertia. Into this period of readjustment, a new breed of entrepreneurs promoting land and water propositions appeared.

The organizers of two such enterprises, the Mission Valley Water Company and the Junipero Land and Water Company, promoted schemes in Mission Valley under the assumption that the San Diego River offered a convenient, accessible source of water they could access. The promoters of these schemes speculated on the sale of appreciated land after they brought water to the property, hence the success of their developments depended on the promise of establishing a conveyance system that supplied water to the land. The major disadvantage became the inability of the company directors to generate enough initial revenue to support the required infrastructure. In the majority of fledgling irrigation districts and private entrepreneurial schemes, the ability to pay for the water service did not materialize until individuals developed the land, so all too often the financial obligations the promoters incurred fell due before the necessary revenues materialized. Nevertheless, in San Diego the lure of perceived profits from placing river water on the abundant undeveloped land overruled reality and inspired the efforts of private entrepreneurs.

In a singular failed venture, Ed Fletcher, local entrepreneur and manager and minority owner of the Cuyamaca Water Company, promoted the construction of a large dam on the upper San Diego River. Fletcher believed that the dam would enhance the overall efficiency of the system, resurrect the company's faltering status and make the enterprise more attractive as a saleable asset. Fletcher's unfulfilled obsession to construct Fletcher Dam permeated the community water conversation for more than twenty years.

The Mission Valley Water Company

In July 1887, almost a year and a half after the Flume Company opened construction, a consortium of San Diego businessmen incorporated the

Mission Valley Water Company (MVWC). The developers saw the agrarian potential of the valley's river floodplain, filed for water rights to irrigate lands in the half-mile-wide valley and offered the sale of $70,000 in bonds to fund their company.

According to California State Engineer William Hammond Hall, the owners ambitiously designed the system to supply irrigation water to a thousand acres of land in Mission Valley. The breadth of this venture made it second only in scope to the San Diego Flume system. In an 1888 report, Hall noted that the project centered on the construction of an eighty-foot-high dam about twelve miles above the mouth of the San Diego River to collect and store the river's winter flow. That distance from downtown placed the dam somewhere in or near Mission Gorge. Hall explained that the masonry dam the company engineers designed would create a long and narrow reservoir with an estimated capacity of 1.5 million gallons of water and, if desired, could be raised another ten feet.[1] The directors hoped to open work on the water system in the fall of 1887.

The organizers designed their scheme around a series of water storage features. From the dammed reservoir, two concrete-lined conduits would convey the water to a series of eight earthen-dammed storage ponds located

With open land and a river as a water source, Mission Valley was an ideal location for private enterprise to attempt to organize land and water ventures in the late 1880s. *CAGen website*.

inside the valley. The main conduit on the south side of the river would branch into two smaller eight-foot-wide-by-four-foot-deep conduits. One conduit would cross to the north side of the river and extend three and a half miles to the reservoir, designated No. 5, and the other would terminate in Reservoir No. 2. Hall also thought that the engineers might install a series of iron pipes to transfer the river water inside the valley to convey water to Old Town and Roseville. The earthen dams at the storage reservoirs, situated at various elevations, ranged in length from sixty feet to seventy feet.[2]

Unfortunately, the project opened in the courtroom, not the field. Within two months of incorporation, the new company governors found themselves in a property dispute with the Junipero Land and Water Company, another venture organizing in the Grantville area at the head of the Mission Valley. At issue was the ownership of some three hundred acres of land in the valley near the Old San Diego Mission. Aware of the progress of the rival San Diego Flume Company, the managers of both the MVWC and the Junipero Company operated with a sense of urgency and quickly settled the matter in court. The Mission Valley managers admittedly viewed the San Diego Flume Company as a business competitor and hoped to have a 2-million-gallon storage reservoir in place and their system in operation before any Flume Company water reached the city.

The organizers of the Mission Valley venture enterprise, like all the private corporations, hoped to bring water to their lands and also contract to sell any excess water to the city. Without supporting evidence, they boasted that in addition to the irrigation application, their system would have the capacity to pull water from the river and pump it to a height where it could supply any portion of the city. In a presentation to the City Water Committee in October 1889, Mr. N.H. Conklin, an attorney and principal stockholder, explained that the MVWC, as designed, would access a catchment much larger than the Flume's that would allow their system to furnish water for the city and the county. Apparently, the company had constructed a dam somewhere. In his address to the City Water Committee, Conklin noted that two members of the water committee had examined the dam and were impressed by it, as the dam was only eight miles east of town, which reduced the cost of pipe required to deliver water to the town. Conklin's statements were a direct challenge to the San Diego Flume to supply the city.[3]

Contemporary engineer Hall expressed doubts about the feasibility of the scheme. On a practical level, irrigating the valley lands for agriculture would not present a serious challenge. But what would be the result? The acreage was limited, the soil barely suitable for farming and the coastal climate not really conducive for large-scale agriculture—all unforeseen reasons why the valley eventually supported limited subsistence farming and large-scale dairy ranching.

The grandiose undertaking never came to fruition. But the scheme was notable as one of the first enterprises to dam the San Diego River to create a supply for downstream users. Presciently, in the early twentieth century, the concept of a dam in the gorge would consume the attention of San Diego city leaders and citizens for the better part of two decades.

THE JUNIPERO LAND AND WATER COMPANY

In March 1887, San Diego civil engineer, county supervisor and real estate promoter Charles J. Fox organized and filed for certification of incorporation for the Junipero Land and Water Company (JLWC). Along with Fox, the original directors of the firm—San Diegans John G. Capron, C.C. Seaman, E.S. Chase and O.S. Hubbell—formed the company "to purchase, own, hold, cultivate, improve, subdivide and sell real property in the County of San Diego."[4] The corporate founders borrowed the familiar first name of Father Junipero Serra, the founder of the Mission San Diego de Alcala, since the mission was located within the confines of the proposed development.

The undeveloped site sat some six miles east of Old Town, situated on land residents had named Grantville in honor of President Ulysses S. Grant. The land sloped gently down to the banks of the San Diego River, where the stream flowed south and then west into the river's wide floodplain in Mission Valley and stood directly west and across the river from the deteriorating Mission San Diego de Alcala. To promote the enterprise, the corporate owners announced that the federal government had selected Grantville as the town site for the first Grand Army of the Republic Soldier's Home in California, a refuge for aging and disabled Civil War veterans.

The organizers opened their promotion with a barrage of advertisements declaring that their location featured the best soil, water and climate in San Diego. The sellers offered prospective buyers daily carriage rides out to the development to view the lots. In February 1888, the company directors announced the completion of the land survey, subdivided the Grantville tract into fifteen- and five-acre parcels and offered the lots for sale at $400 per acre.

As with all early San Diego land ventures, an available water supply was essential to the JLWC's success. From the beginning of the Junipero promotion, the company directors guaranteed a steady water supply and created the impression that a water system was in place and ready to serve new buyers, and workmen were also laying pipes to distribute water throughout the tract. In reality, the development had more promises than water.

Fox and his associates touted a water system that did not exist. The organizers guaranteed water, but not necessarily from their system. It was undoubtedly a bittersweet moment when the Junipero directors announced in May 1887 that the water for the new development would come from the San Diego Flume Company, not their system. The agreement with the Flume Company owners granted a perpetual supply of domestic and irrigation water to the Junipero tracts at a price yet to be determined.

The community of Grantville eventually took shape, but without the Army Home or the irrigated fields the Junipero promoters envisioned. The lack of a water system doomed the enterprise. The Flume Company project failed to materialize, and faced with increasingly pressing financial obligations, the Junipero promotion collapsed in 1909.

Fletcher Dam

From the turn of the twentieth century, Ed Fletcher was a prominent figure in the San Diego water scene. He was part owner and the manager of the Cuyamaca Water Company, intimately involved in the San Diego River water rights struggle, a strident advocate for a dam in Mission Gorge and an ardent opponent of a dam at El Capitan. While Fletcher wove his way through the myriad water affairs, he orchestrated an ambitious river project to place a large dam on the upper San Diego River. Over the course of twenty years, his dream morphed from an aspiration into an obsession.

In one of his first tasks as the manager of the new CWC, Fletcher investigated ways the company could increase the amount of water withdrawn from the San Diego River. The existing diverting dam was simply too small. With this in mind, Fletcher ordered his engineers to devise a plan for creating a series of upstream diversion dams and storage reservoirs to provide a more consistent flow into the system. In March 1911, William S. Post, the chief engineer for the CWC, investigated twelve possible dam and reservoir sites on the river upstream from El Cajon Mountain. Post favored locations on a westward-flowing tributary of King Creek and a site on Boulder Creek above the CWC diversion dam.[5] Over the next two years, Fletcher and Murray pondered the idea but realized that the company was not financially able to act.

Regardless of the drawbacks, by 1916 Fletcher was fully engaged in the concept of his new dam—named, of course, Fletcher Dam. Fletcher wanted to construct the dam in the narrow mountain canyon Post recommended about a mile upstream from the existing diverting dam and closer to the river's source. Dam designer John Eastwood assured Fletcher that a 230-foot-tall multiple-arch dam at this elevation would safely and efficiently deliver by gravity flow the water through the flume system to the city's distribution system. Fletcher

John S. Eastwood designed a 160-foot-tall multi-arch structure for Fletcher's dam on the upper river. *From Structurae, the International Database and Gallery of Structures.*

myopically ignored the challenge of passing the water through a decaying system, the cost of engineering, constructing an additional twelve miles of conveyance infrastructure and the cost of the dam.

In his determination to build the dam, Fletcher lobbied the federal government, the State of California and the city. In April 1916, he contacted Secretary of the Interior Franklin Lane and requested Lane's assurance that the federal government would not interfere with the construction of the new dam. Fletcher told Lane that the State Railroad Commission had already approved the plans for the structure and state engineers had agreed to supervise the construction. He also contended that the dam would benefit the Capitan Grande Reservation Indians as a flood control structure and increase the domestic and irrigation water supply to the reservation. In a 1918 meeting before the Common Council, he argued that the new dam would leave any downstream structure at El Capitan with a more than adequate watershed. As an enticement, Fletcher proposed to relinquish rights to his portion of the site property at El Capitan if the city approved the project. While Lane demurred, City Engineer George Cromwell explained that the dam at the location Fletcher indicated would deplete 40 percent of the river's flow in a normal year and that in a dry year, the dam would adversely affect the flow to the proposed city system at El Capitan. Members

Fletcher planned to construct his namesake dam immediately upstream from the Flume system's diverting dam. *City of San Diego Office of City Clerk, Archives and Records Management.*

of the Common Council declared that they would fight the water company to the "last ditch" on the matter.[6]

Fletcher expended considerable time, money and effort to keep his vision alive. In 1918, his engineers conducted drilling on several sites near Boulder Creek, and the results encouraged Fletcher to purchase 160 acres around the creek and apply to the War Finance Commission for a loan to develop the site. He also continued to badger city officials to approve his project. He preached to city leaders and the community at large that the El Capitan project remained uncertain, was too expensive and was years away from implementation even if voters approved it, while his new dam was a cost-effective alternative.

Murray's death in 1921 released Fletcher from the majority owner's authoritarian grip and allowed Fletcher more latitude to pursue the project. In 1922, Fletcher authorized Eastwood to conduct more core drilling at the site near Boulder Creek. Eastwood ascertained that the bedrock formations were sufficient for a large dam, which encouraged Fletcher to beseech city bureaucrats to allow him to open construction on a multi-arch dam that Eastwood could have in place within six months. As a further inducement, Fletcher promised to supply San Diego with all the excess

Fletcher envisioned a structure similar to the Eastwood-designed multiple-arch Hodges Dam, constructed in 1918. *City of San Diego Water Department Archive.*

water the dam collected at a low rate. Fletcher conveniently ignored the fact that city water officials understood that his dam would adversely affect the plans for any downstream dams on the river either in Mission Gorge or at El Capitan. Throughout Fletcher's quest, Eastwood avidly supported his mentor, yet as a professional engineer, he conceded in a 1922 report that Fletcher Dam reservoir would only have one-sixth the capacity of a reservoir at El Capitan.

Into the late 1920s, as the city rebuffed and the public evinced indifference to his dam, Fletcher clung to his vision. In early 1929, he publicized that local water engineer Fredrick E. Green included Fletcher Dam as an essential element in his comprehensive river plan and insisted that any river plan must include Fletcher Dam in the opening phase before an El Capitan or San Vincente project. In his urgency to promote the dam, Fletcher also contracted the services of the Hollywood Movie Supply Company to take photos of the dam site and create "cleverly faked shots" to show the completed dam with a reservoir filled with sparking mountain water.[7] At one point, Fletcher became so enamored of the project that he appeared ready to abandon his Mission Gorge enterprise to concentrate on the construction of his namesake dam.

For twenty years, financial, geographic and political realities forestalled Fletcher's visionary dam project until the onus of construction costs, the uncertain future of the CWC, the speculative nature of placing a large dam on a small catchment and the 1924 plebiscite to construct El Capitan Dam ultimately doomed Fletcher's vision.

The Legacy of the Failed Ventures

Promoting a private water venture in San Diego in the decades surrounding the turn of the twentieth century required diligent management and an understanding of the complexities and realities of operating a water enterprise in a water-challenged region. The unreliable coastal rainfall determined that the success of the Mission Valley and Junipero ventures hinged on water management plans that took water from the San Diego River—not an easy task in drought-plagued San Diego, where water managers faced the problem of promised distribution amounts in times of water shortage. The ease of promotion belied the difficulty of actually conveying water to the lands. These for-profit ventures generally defaulted because of financial instability, flawed leadership and the failure to secure the guaranteed water supply. Privatization became a cost-to-benefit circumstance. The tipping point came when the value and possibility of securing water overtook the advantages and cost to maintain the venture.

To become the principal water supplier to the City of San Diego was the ultimate goal of any water venture. The company that managed to introduce an adequate water supply to the city would overwhelm its rivals. But early private water endeavors simply did not have that capacity. Even the San Diego Flume Company, which functioned into the 1930s, failed to solve the town's perpetual "water question" and for almost forty years disappointed founders and investors alike until the La Mesa, Lemon Grove and Spring Valley Irrigation District acquired the enterprise.

The private corporations did benefit the San Diego hydraulic community. The engineers the developers hired investigated the interior watersheds, drafted plans and specifications, drew maps, created cost estimates and took the data, reports and recommendations back to their company directors. They disseminated the information to other professionals, which revealed the physical and financial extent of potential projects, served as templates for subsequent water endeavors and promoted the feasibility of dam construction on the county's rivers. More than any other factor, the engagement of private water companies, including the San Diego Flume Company, revealed that water service to urbanized areas was inherently a public undertaking. Urban water systems required complicated infrastructure and long-term planning, with the expectation of slow and small return on the investment. It was a matter of service. A private concern would not necessarily operate with the best interest of the community in mind, whereas a municipal water system prioritized service over profit. In San Diego, a private water enterprise proved a poor match for serving the public need. Perhaps the most important lesson from the failures of the private companies was the realization that the city must be prepared to invest in its future. Private capitalists did not have that capacity or commitment.

Like the Mission Valley and Junipero enterprises, Fletcher's dam project was a private venture, but one with considerable more structure and administrative support. But despite Fletcher's backing, reputation and enthusiasm, the vagaries of the project made it a questionable project from the beginning. Fletcher certainly realized that the construction of this dam would force the city to reconsider any El Capitan project. A dam the size Fletcher projected on the upper river, in the location he favored, would make an El Capitan dam less viable. Opposition from the city was a given. On the other hand, because of the large watershed downstream of the Fletcher site and its location upstream of Mission Gorge, the Fletcher Dam would exert less effect on a gorge dam. In the end, no matter the depth of Fletcher's personal commitment, reality in the form of financial, political and geographic obstacles condemned his dream dam.

Chapter 6

EARLY DAMS ON THE RIVER

The conservation of water is merely the application of man's ingenuity,
backed by the necessary capital.
—*John D. Spreckels, San Diego businessman, 1929*

The earliest dams on the San Diego River, the Franciscan's Old Mission Dam and the San Diego Flume Company's diverting dam, were simple structures that reflected the pragmatic nature of the builders. The designers of these dams selected sites that would accommodate a structure within the skills of the builders, were accessible to workers and featured construction materials readily available in the surrounding area. These were modest dams with small reservoirs to store and dispense the collected water. These dams captured water from the river's seasonal flow in the time of high flow, or during floods, and were small enough that floodwaters would flow over the crest and not damage the structure. These elemental structures were the only dams on the San Diego River until the completion of El Capitan Dam in 1934.

THE MISSION DAM

The development of the San Diego River began with the construction of the Mission Dam in the early nineteenth century. The destiny of the Alta California mission the Franciscan Fathers founded in San Diego in 1769 depended on the ability of the padres to cultivate crops and the capacity of the nearby river to supply irrigation water. In the first decade of San Diego's existence, consecutive years of drought revealed the river's capricious nature and forced the padres to reevaluate their circumstances. The priests consulted with their superiors and, on the advice of Spanish colonial governor Viceroy Burcareli y Vruca, relocated their primitive adobe mission in 1774 to a site with better soil and closer to the river and the native population. Father Francisco Palou, Father Junipero Serra's adjunct, noted that the new location several miles upstream coincided with Bucareli's earlier prophetic instruction for the fathers to construct *"una firme represa,"* a solid or sturdy dam, across the river to provide water for the citizens of the future pueblo.[1]

Thirty years later, the padres fulfilled Bucareli's vision with the construction of the dam that became the core of the first European irrigation project in Alta California and the first significant man-made water feature on the river. Between 1803 and 1814, the Franciscan priests supervised the construction of an intricate aqueduct-irrigation system fed from a small, dammed reservoir. The system supplied river water for the adjacent irrigated fields, grazing livestock and for domestic use in the hot, dry summer months. Frederick Green, a local self-educated authority on the Mission Dam, perused the Franciscans' mission records and averred that, curiously, the documents only refer to the aqueduct and made no mention of a dam. In his 1933 study, Green surmised that the priests evidently considered the dam as a part of the aqueduct and gave it no special mention. The aqueduct was an extensive and complex undertaking that required years to design and build and required three times the materials and labor used for the construction of the rudimentary dam.[2]

The fathers selected an excellent site for the dam. The 220-foot-wide-by-12-foot-high cobblestone, brick, mortar and concrete structure sat at the head of a gorge some five miles north and east of the mission. The selection of the dam site suggested some engineering awareness. There were sites closer to the mission that displayed solid bedrock and good sidewalls, but all required a taller dam and featured narrower approaches that made any structure susceptible to damage from flooding. The priests chose a location where the low dam fit into the exposed bedrock, and the westward-flowing river fed the water from a long approach over a wide, flat river plain. To maintain a constant, gradual descent, the elaborate ceramic tile–lined aqueduct crossed over a series of stone trestles. Green stressed that the aqueduct, not the dam, was the essential element in the irrigation system and posited that

In 1813, the Franciscan padres constructed the Mission Dam to collect and distribute water into the mission's irrigation system. *Author's collection.*

it was possible that a smaller dam or temporary dam preceded the gorge structure by several years. Green believed the padres probably constructed the dam at the end of the aqueduct project or immediately thereafter. With the completion of the dam, the padres unknowingly instituted the region's legacy of damming rivers to create reservoirs.

The fact that a religious institution engineered and constructed a diversion dam and an extensive aqueduct delivery system left Green no doubt that experienced Spanish engineers, already in California, were probably involved in the design and construction of the project. Spanish colonial engineers had already constructed hundreds of dams and irrigation systems throughout Mexico, hence the process was not unique to the Alta California Mission. Green surmised that the level of masonry work at the mission had advanced to the point that the construction of a stone dam was definitely within the purview of the Catholic padres and the Native Americans, but also he thought Alta California governor Diego de Borcia might have sent skilled artisans to assist on the project. He believed that the Indians were largely responsible for gathering lime for hillside deposits, kiln-drying the material to create the essential mortar, gathering the best clay from the river bottoms for adobe tiles and working in the brick tile works.[3]

The Mission Dam has withstood the ravages of time and nature remarkably well. The twelve-foot-wide floodgate on the northern end of the dam performed as designed and protected the structure from recurring floodwaters. In his 1933 study, Green estimated that after decades without maintenance and being overtopped by ten feet in the 1916 flood, then surviving the floods of 1921 and 1927, the dam was 85 percent intact. Green credited the dam's longevity to the type of rock selected and the manner in which the laborers performed the masonry work. Local lore related that after the secularization of the missions in the 1830s, there was no motivation to maintain the structure or the aqueduct, and both fell into disrepair into the 1860s. Locals refurbished the dam and briefly brought it back into service in the 1870s.

Mission Dam now resides within the Mission Trails Regional Park, a city facility, as a protected State of California Historical Landmark. It was seventy-five years after the completion of Mission Dam before the next major project appeared on the river.

THE SAN DIEGO FLUME DIVERTING DAM

Following the organization of the San Diego Flume Company in May 1886, Theodore S. Van Dyke and his business associates placed the next significant man-made feature on the river. Van Dyke's speculative enterprise hinged on the availability of water and transporting that water to consumers. To overcome the deficiencies of the Flume's area of operation, a locality with an inconsistent seasonal flow and one prone to lengthy droughts, Van Dyke planned to construct a small dam on the upper river. He designed the dam to collect and feed water into the wooden flume and transport it some thirty miles downstream to the city distribution network. Van Dyke's first task was to identify a suitable site for the dam.

For months, Van Dyke and his engineers wandered the narrow upper river valley in search of suitable dam sites. They considered drilling a tunnel through the hillside above the site local dwellers called Rocky Bar and building a dam where the tunnel joined the river. Van Dyke initially thought that building the dam at this upper site would save money and create a better diversion system, but after consideration, he calculated that the location required the construction of a more expensive structure, and while a dam at that elevation would increase the downstream grade, it would not enhance the system's flow. Van Dyke and his crew also examined a potential locale in Dye Canyon at the head of the river but eventually dismissed the idea as impractical. After months of exploration, Van Dyke settled on the site at Rocky Bar.

The site was situated in a high, flat mountain valley with a narrow outlet, a perfect dam site. Van Dyke described Rocky Bar as an open canyon flanked by barren rugged and steep mountain slopes at 810 feet of elevation, which meant that the stream fell at a rate of about 30 feet per mile. Van Dyke recognized the location's limitations, but given the options, he and his engineers believed that it offered the best opportunity for success.[4]

The Rocky Bar dam site sat at the confluence of the southward-coursing San Diego River and a westward-flowing tributary called Boulder Creek. The placement of the dam at the outfall of the creek, which dropped from the east some four thousand feet of elevation over twelve miles, allowed the system to supplement the river's capricious, seasonal output. To supplement the uneven flow of the river, Van Dyke purchased property containing a seasonal wet meadow at the headwaters of Boulder Creek. Where the creek departed the meadow, Van Dyke built a low earth-filled dam to create a reservoir to collect and regulate water. The Spanish-influenced nineteenth-century Native Americans called the wetland where Van Dyke built the dam *Laguna Que Se Seca*, freely translated as the "wet place that dries up." The Flume owners soon discovered the significance of the name.

Van Dyke opened construction on the dam he called Cuyamaca Dam in September 1887 and immediately encountered a complication. He did not anticipate that as the reservoir filled, water would flood portions of the adjoining Stonewall Gold Mine, property owned by California Governor Robert Waterman. Waterman became aware of Van Dyke's plans and protested that the reservoir might inundate the mine and other parts of his land and demanded that the Flume operators halt the project. The Flume owners responded with a lawsuit condemning six hundred acres of Waterman's land. After Waterman lost several court appeals, he settled for $45,000 in damages, and the Flume engineers started construction of the thirty-five-foot-tall dam in September 1887 and completed it in February 1888.

With Cuyamaca Dam underway, Van Dyke began construction on the river dam. It was a simple, practical masonry dam constructed on a straight line across the river. The dam featured two control wheels on the crest, which operated the wooden-planked release gates. Van Dyke's design placed two culverts running through the masonry structure to allow workers to

Theodore Van Dyke constructed Cuyamaca Dam in 1886 to create a reservoir to supplement the river's flow into the Flume system. *City of San Diego Water Department Archive.*

drain accumulated sediment from the reservoir basin when necessary. The engineers designed the reservoir to feed only the amount of water into the flume that it could accept at peak use. A dedicated outlet on the east end of the dam directed water into the flume chute, while another outlet released any overflow back into the downstream river channel. The designers believed that in high water events, the dam's location on the upper river and its low profile would allow the surging water to sweep over the flat crest with little or no damage. For whatever reason, the Flume operators never bestowed an official name on the dam but simply referred to it as the diverting dam. When State Engineer Hammond Hall called the structure the San Diego Diverting Dam in his 1888 report, the name became accepted.

The diverting dam was not exceptional even by late nineteenth-century standards. The structure measured just over 34 feet high and 447 feet long, with a 5-foot-wide crest. The dam rested on a foundation sunk 10 to 12 feet into the rocky riverbed. Workers quarried the necessary stone and fill material from the rocky riverbed and adjacent slopes and freighted in 2,410 bags of concrete to affix the rocks. Supplies arrived from San Diego via the dirt Eagle Peak Road, which paralleled the river as it ran north and east from Lakeside toward Julian. Engineers on the job included R.H. Stretch, Lou B.

Harris and J.M. Graham, with consultation from civic engineers Hall and James D. Schuyler and local hydrologist Clarence S. Alverson. Estimates on the cost of construction of the dam vary, according to the sources, from $50,000 to $54,000. Given the distance from San Diego and the condition of the wagon road, workers camped at the site throughout the five-month project, probably on the gentle rise immediately east of the dam site where the owners added a caretaker's cottage in 1889.

The dam proved to be an extremely leaky structure. Upon completion, the engineers tested the structure and discovered that the instability of soft granite footing led to excessive seepage. On the advice of the engineers, Van Dyke ordered the upper face stripped to the foundation and then applied a two-foot-thick covering or "apron" of masonry from the crest to six feet below the foundation and plastered and painted the face.[5] The owners accepted the necessity of the improvements, an estimated $5,000, to make the system functional. After these renovations, the small Flume dam underwent only minor renovations over the next twenty years.

After Murray and Fletcher purchased the Flume system in 1910, they requested a report on the condition of the dam. William Post, the CWC's chief engineer, surveyed the dam and reported back to Fletcher in October 1911. Post noted a "washout" in the foundation on the backside of the dam

San Diego Flume Company engineers designed a small masonry dam on the upper river to feed water into the wooden Flume system. *City of San Diego Water Department Archive.*

The Flume operators strengthened the exterior of the small diverting dam and eventually built a cottage for the dam keepers. *City of San Diego Water Department Archive.*

and observed that the natural level of the ground by the reservoir's west side spillway allowed water to escape the reservoir. He recommended the owners wrap the front of the dam with a water-tight apron to avoid future undermining and that they raise the dam five feet to achieve the reservoir's maximum capacity—any higher, he argued, would be a waste of money. Prophetically, Post said that the work should be performed in the summer, when the dam was usually out of service until the rainy season. Murray accepted the suggestions and ordered the dam raised another five feet, the exterior slurried with concrete to fortify the structure and ordered the engineers to reconfigure the spillways to make them more efficient.[6]

The epic 1916 flood overtopped the diverting dam, but the structure's low profile and its location on the upper river saved it from any severe damage. The 1927 flood, however, broke through the eastern abutment of the forty-year-old dam and necessitated significant renovations. Along with those repairs, the engineers placed three concrete and masonry buttresses on the dam's downstream side to strengthen the structure. Today, the dam stands largely as engineers configured it in the late 1920s. The dam is situated on City of San Diego property, but the Helix Water District maintains and administers the structure.

In the late 1920s, the La Mesa Irrigation District upgraded the outlet apparatus that regulated water from the diverting dam into the wooden flume. *Author's collection.*

THE EARLY DAMS

Until the completion of El Capitan Dam in 1934, the San Diego was a free-flowing river, as neither the Mission Dam nor the diverting dam hindered the river's natural flow. But the builders of these modest dams did not intend them as conservation structures. They were limited in scope and designed for specific purposes. By the twentieth century, the tiny Mission Dam on the lower river had become nonfunctional, and the San Diego Flume diverting dam, located high on the upper river, did little to restrain the flow of the river. Both were mere artificial obstacles in flood events.

Chapter 7

THE RIVER'S HIDDEN RESOURCE

[Y]ou ought to get hold of some pumping lands.
It is your only salvation in case of a dry season.
—*William S. Post, Cuyamaca Water Company Engineer, 1913*

When the Europeans arrived to colonize the area that became San Diego in the summer of 1769, the weather was undoubtedly hot and dry. The first task for the crew of the exhausted, half-starved Spanish adventurers was to secure drinking water. Apparently, the local natives, the Kumeyaays, likely from their village of Cosoy near the bay, escorted the Europeans along the worn shoreline path (the La Playa Trail) that crossed the sandy and grassy flat and led the thirsty Spaniards to the nearby river valley. Generally, by midsummer, with the onset of the dry season, the river was typically little more than a sluggish creek if not completely dry, and the majority of the Kumeyaays had migrated upstream following the receding river. The natives who remained in the dry river valley knew from their collective experience that the river held a hidden water source. Like their predecessors, the American San Diegans learned that reliance on the periodic surface flow of the San Diego River was a problematic venture and that even in dry times, the sandy riverbed concealed unseen water reserves.

Surface and groundwater appear separate, but in the San Diego River, they shared a common source and were interdependent. While surface water flowed above ground, groundwater percolated laterally and downward through layers of soil and sand and accumulated in the riverbed in natural underground spaces called aquifers. Like surface water, groundwater was a limited resource, and the supply fluctuated depending on the amount withdrawn and the river's capacity to recharge the supply. In nineteenth-century California, groundwater rights came with landownership. If an individual had access to an underground field, that individual had the right to drill and pump water without limitations. Until the State of California started to regulate groundwater in the twenty-first century, the lack of a regulatory authority created a state of water anarchy that was essentially a "water free-for-all."[1]

The development of the San Diego River was really a tale of two rivers. While city leaders struggled with the incumbent issues of developing the river's surface waters, subsurface waters sustained municipal consumers and upstream ranchers and kept private river enterprises solvent. In water-challenged San Diego, the cycle of droughts and the resulting ephemeral nature of the San Diego River, combined with increased consumer demand and the town's uncertain water supply, made the use of river groundwater an essential element in the city's water agenda.

The City Supply

San Diego's climatic conditions determined the river's flow and rendered securing surface river water a seasonal affair. As a result, between the 1850s and the 1870s, San Diego's townspeople relied primarily on water pumped from subterranean wells dug in the San Diego River near Old Town and artesian wells on San Diego Mesa, not the river's surface flow. The mesa-topped walls of the river valley enclosed about six square miles of the gravel and sand riverine water fields that created the Mission Valley aquifer. The aquifer followed the San Diego River from the southern end of Mission Gorge west through the valley to the outfall at False Bay.

American water seekers quickly discovered that the groundwater table in the riverbed around Old Town was relatively shallow, which made it possible to dig pits in the sandy, gravel riverbed and extract the accumulated water. The process of creating a water hole in the riverbed had changed little since the Spanish and Mexican eras. Workers hand-shoveled a pit through the layer of sand, gravel and loosely consolidated conglomerates of the riverbed and sided the pit with thin wood planks. As the demand for water increased, the wells grew deeper and more sophisticated. The well diggers replaced the wood planks with adobe bricks or ceramic tile and replaced the buckets with pumps. The techniques had changed, but the need for groundwater remained constant.

Private individuals drilled the first commercial wells in the riverbed north of Old Town in the early 1870s. The relocation of the center of town from Old Town to the harbor side New Town in the 1870s required pumping water out of Mission Valley and lifting it to the city storage and distribution reservoirs on San Diego Mesa. The commercial opportunities encouraged the San Diego Water Company to incorporate in 1873 as the town's earliest private water enterprise. The company took water from a well near Pound Canyon, which fed two concrete reservoirs on San Diego Mesa. But the limited capacity of the Pound Canyon well and the increasing demands for water led the company owners to sink additional wells in the Mission Valley riverbed. By 1875, the company was taking the majority of water it supplied to the city from wells in the lands in the valley below today's Presidio Hill. The company owners later laid a pipeline along the lower, northward-facing portion of the San Diego Mesa and pumped water from wells to the crest of the San Diego Mesa at University Heights. To mitigate the costs, the company tunneled through the valley wall and built an aqueduct to convey the water to the town's distribution reservoir at 5th and Hawthorne. In the late 1880s, the company routinely pumped river groundwater to the 4-million-gallon San Diego Reservoir located on the hill above Old Town. The company's limited resources, however, made it difficult to serve the growing town's water needs.

The lower-than-normal rainy season in the winter of 1902 forced city water managers to rethink the town's supply system. The City Water Department purchased what water was available from the San Diego Flume Company and other private sources, but that failed to meet demand. To cover the shortfall, the superintendent of the City Water Department, Clarence S. Alverson, suggested the city expand its underground fields in Mission Valley. Alverson was confident that the groundwater in the riverbed was sufficient to meet the city's needs. To prove his point, in June 1902, Alverson led the members of the City Water Committee, members of the Board of Public Works, the city attorney and the city engineer on a trip to the Mission Valley fields. The group inspected the Mission Valley pumping plants and discussed the possibility of installing additional auxiliary pumps to extract more water and purchasing more private land if required. City leaders heeded Alverson's advice and over the next ten years enlarged the Mission Valley underground operations.[2]

From the 1890s, pumping plants in Mission Valley extracted river groundwater for city use. *San Diego History Center.*

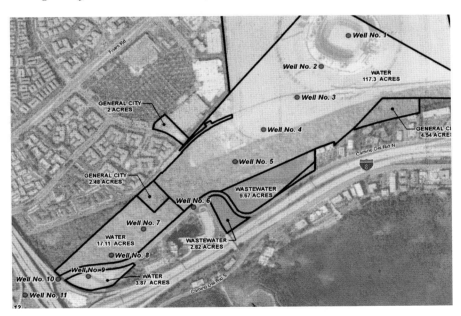

By 1913, the city was operating twelve plants to pump groundwater from Mission Valley. *San Diego City Public Utilities Department.*

The city and private parties used steam pumps to draw water from riverbed wells in El Monte Valley. *City of San Diego Water Department Archive.*

The city eventually owned and managed a series of riverbed fields that extended from Old Town east to just below the site of the Old Mission. To increase efficiency, the city also installed larger, more powerful pumps, contracted to drill deeper wells and connected existing wells to a main pumping station to increase the water flow. By 1914, the field included twelve wells that varied in depth from forty to eighty feet and pumped the river groundwater into a concrete sump then lifted the water three hundred feet to the University Heights Reservoir. This field functioned as the city's primary source of drinking water from 1914 to 1936, a year after the city completed El Capitan Dam.

Given the amount of groundwater the city pumped, the town's water experts worried that the rate of extraction might deplete the Mission Valley riverbeds. Unsure of the capacity of the fields and aware that the settlers and ranchers in the El Cajon Valley had tapped the underground source stored in the river valley on their lands for decades, city watermen looked upriver to augment the city supply. In early October 1904, a group of twenty-five water hunters—including Mayor Frank Fray, the City Water Committee members and members of assorted local civic improvement clubs—traveled east to El Cajon Valley to investigate those underground fields. The travel party wandered eastward up the river valley and held a luncheon meeting with several of the El Cajon Valley landowners. The farmers and ranchers pointed out the best sites for accessing groundwater and appeared eager to sell their water-bearing land. The outing convinced the assemblage of the underground water potential in El Cajon Valley and prompted Mayor Fray to request the Common Council to investigate how the city might access the source.[3]

On October 31, 1904, the Common Council passed an ordinance that called for city engineers to determine a site in the El Cajon Valley that the city could acquire and install a pumping plant. (In the early 1900s, the area called the El Cajon Valley vaguely applied to the entire El Cajon Basin, from Santee to El Monte, which included the San Diego River Valley that bordered the valley's northern edge.) The council signed Alverson to a ten-day contract to work under the supervision of the City Water Committee for fifteen dollars per day. Alverson accepted the task but cautioned the councilmen that his results might be skewed as the investigation came at the end of an eight-year period that featured light rainfall, which meant groundwater levels might be lower than normal. He ordered twelve wells drilled and installed three pumping stations to determine the extent of the subterranean water in the area. In November 1904, Alverson reported to the council that, in his opinion, the fields contained a large quantity of water, and with the fields only twelve to fifteen miles from the city distribution reservoir, the city could pump and convey the groundwater at a reasonable expenditure. Alverson estimated that the purchase of the appropriate lands and the installation of pumps and conduits would cost the city $350,000, an amount he felt the municipality could recoup within six years.[4]

Alverson's encouraging report and the lingering effects of the seven-year drought motivated the councilmen to send Alverson back to the valley three

The city drew the bulk of its water from the groundwater basins in Mission Valley and the San Diego River Valley. *San Diego City Public Utilities Department.*

months later. From his collected data, he recommended the city construct a dammed reservoir near the head of the groundwater works to allow the collected water to gravity-flow to the city system. Alverson also optimistically suggested that the city enlarge the reservoir at University Heights in anticipation of the increased supply.

In late 1904, the directors of the pro-growth chamber of commerce consulted with the council to conduct a parallel study. It was not uncommon for the chamber, the influential association of the town's most prominent men, to intervene in a city venture. On this occasion, the chamber directors consulted with the Common Council and agreed to engage prominent Los Angeles water engineer John B. Lippincott (who had worked for the City of Los Angeles on the Owens Valley project) as a consulting engineer. The council paid Lippincott's wages and authorized him to examine the possibility of securing water from the bottomlands of the San Diego River in the El Cajon Valley. In December 1904, Lippincott conducted a two-day, fourteen-mile-long investigation from the community of Lakeside north to the San Diego Flume Company's diverting dam. Lippincott concurred with Alverson's assessment that the area held a natural underground reservoir, and in his January 1905 report to the Special Water Committee of the Common Council, he recommended the installation of several pumping plants and a gravity-flow conduit to connect the water-bearing land to the University Heights Reservoir. Without hesitation, Lippincott asserted that the project was commercially and physically feasible and that the city should purchase the riverfront acres on which the city currently held options and construct the system as promptly as possible.[5]

Left: Local hydrologist Clarence Alverson surveyed the river and determined that the city could survive on underground water from the interior valley. *City of San Diego Water Department Archive.*

Right: The chamber of commerce hired water engineer Joseph B. Lippincott to come to San Diego and survey the possibilities of underground water in the middle river valley. *Water Resource Center Archive.*

The Alverson and Lippincott reports convinced municipal leaders that accessing the water-bearing lands along the San Diego River in the El Cajon Valley was both fiscally viable and an efficient way to supplement the city water system. Funding the project, however, required a public mandate. To that end, the council placed a measure on the 1905 municipal ballot that sought approval to purchase land in the El Cajon Valley. Presciently, the negative response and the partisan rhetoric foreshadowed the polarizing division of future water bond issues. Rather than concentrating on the need for additional water, the sides were divided over minor technical aspects and the cost of the project and turned a well-intended project into a divisive issue. The *Union* lamented the "shameless campaigning" that resulted in a no vote on the proposition.[6]

The councilmen accepted the initiative's failure and then unilaterally began improving the Mission Valley groundwater program. In January

1906, the council approved funds for new wells. Water engineer Alverson applauded the move and offered his opinion that additional Mission Valley wells would reduce the city's reliance on domestic water from the inconsistent Flume Company and would make more water available for inland irrigation users. Municipal expansionists, largely members of the chamber, fully agreed and urged the city to aggressively continue efforts to develop underground resources.

In their urgency to stabilize the town's water system, the chamber leaders preempted the council again and in early 1913 reengaged Lippincott to evaluate the city's groundwater capabilities. Lippincott reported to the chamber membership in August that the city possessed one hundred acres of water-bearing lands in Mission Valley and had expended more than $185,000 to place twelve plants, dispersed on an east–west axis through the center of the valley, in operation. Given the scope of the town's existing groundwater resources and the fact that the city was enjoying above-normal rainfall, the directors stemmed their urgency and adopted a more measured approach in developing the river.

In September 1916, Alverson received another opportunity to advance his underground water advocacy when local rancher J. Johnson hired him to investigate the underground water potential on his riverside property near Riverview. Alverson again wandered the river from its source in the mountains to the Old Mission Dam. This investigation convinced Alverson to deviate from the current consensus that favored large dams and associated reservoirs and postulate that the potential yield from underground river water was a more reliable water source than an artificial storage reservoir. Alverson estimated that fourteen thousand acre-feet of groundwater existed between Riverview and Old Mission Dam and concluded that these resources on Johnson's property alone could furnish the city 7.5 million gallons of water per day. Alverson urged the city to acquire these properties.[7] As the chamber, the council and city water managers debated Alverson's recommendations, the epic flood of January 1916 interceded.

The flood filled the county's reservoirs but also swept away the city's twelve groundwater wells in Mission Valley. A vital element of the town's water supply disappeared in days. The loss of the wells, pumps and collecting lines shut off the water supply and ultimately amounted to more than $20,000 in damages. The importance of the wells compelled Manager of City Operations Fred Lockwood to submit a request to the Common Council for funds to rebuild the flood-damaged wells and pumps and called on the council to order city crews to work around the clock to return the river pumping plants to full operation. The impact of the loss compelled the Common Council to approve funds to protect the valley wells against future flood events. In November 1916, city engineers constructed wooden V-shaped safety guards on the upstream side of the pumps and drove three-inch-thick wooden planks twenty-four feet into the riverbed to secure the protective devices.[8] The council realized that the wells were simply too valuable to leave unprotected.

The operation of the groundwater plants in Mission Valley caused a minor bureaucratic stir in September 1920. Charles Sumner, the president of the City Water Commission, unilaterally ordered the plants shut down over a budgetary disagreement. Sumner told the members of the Common Council that they, not his agency, should be funding the operation of the plants. The councilmen, concerned how the loss of the plants might affect the city supply, ordered Sumner to resume pumping operations immediately or face an investigation. The need for water trumped the internecine disagreement. Sumner acquiesced, and the plants reopened operations within days.

In 1929, local hydrologist Frederick Green, a former employee of the U.S. Coast and Geodetic Survey, revisited the groundwater issue. Green compiled a detailed document on past groundwater use and the potential development of the fourteen-mile strip of the river valley that extended north from the Old Mission Dam to the proposed El Capitan dam site. Green studied old surveys and spent weeks investigating along the river. Like Alverson and Lippincott, Green agreed that these lands were a valuable source for subsurface water. In Green's estimation, these water storage gravels represented at least 11 percent of the river's total yield of the river. Green cautioned that the construction of a large dam on the river could reduce the gallons per day yield from the fields from 3 million to 1 million and that the continued pumping at the El Monte gravel basin would reduce the water table in the lower groundwater basins and restrict the replenishment of the beds.[9] Green urged city leaders to expend the necessary funds to develop the water-bearing lands in the upper San Diego River Basins at Riverview and El Monte. Months later, the council ordered San Diego city engineer George Cromwell to conduct a similar study, which confirmed Green's findings.

The data Green and Cromwell gathered indicated that from 1897 into the late 1920s, the city, except in the years between 1907 and 1913, had relied heavily on water drawn from the pumping plants in Mission Valley and periodic uses of the Riverview and the El Monte plants. From 1916 to 1928, the Cuyamaca Water Company and the city system pumped an average of 1,655 acre-feet of water per year from the San Diego River Valley and Mission Valley Basins, which amounted to approximately 1.5 million gallons daily. In 1925, the Mission Valley Pumping Plant alone produced 251,959 thousands of gallons of water to the city. River groundwater was clearly an integral element in the city water supply.

THE SAN DIEGO FLUME COMPANY AND THE CUYAMACA WATER COMPANY

From 1888 to 1897, the steady flow of the San Diego River allowed the operators of the San Diego Flume Company to rely on surface water to drive their water system. However, a protracted drought extending into 1898 diminished the river's surface water and forced the owners to seek alternative water sources and install the first underground pumping facilities in the river valley near El Monte. That fall, Flume engineers drilled thirty-seven wells in the gravel riverbed and placed steam-powered extraction pumps. The El Monte fields proved remarkably productive. The fields produced more than 5 million gallons of groundwater in five months of operation in 1898 and almost 240 million gallons in 1899. Groundwater kept the Flume Company in operation.[10]

Interestingly, Green observed in his 1929 study that during the pronounced drought from 1898 to 1904, the amount of groundwater the Flume Company drew from the El Cajon Valley basin was actually quite modest. Perhaps the cash-strapped Flume owners were hesitant to invest in expanding the groundwater operations of an enterprise they hoped to sell. Nevertheless, the productivity of the groundwater program allowed the Flume Company to survive until the return of normal rainfall in 1905. From 1905 to 1912, the surface flow of the river and water from Cuyamaca Lake was sufficient to meet supply demands, and the operators of the Flume pumped no groundwater into the system. Then came the drought of 1913.

The severe drought conditions that started in 1912 induced the new Flume owners, James Murray and Ed Fletcher, to resume underground pumping operations. With the company's credibility as a major supplier to the city at stake, the owners returned to the San Diego River beds in the El Monte Basin, ordered scores of new wells drilled, installed steam-powered pumps to lift the collected water into transmission reservoirs and levied a surcharge to consumers to cover their expenses. Consumers appreciated the improvements but protested the increased rates.

The State Railroad Commission responded to the consumer complaints with a series of hearings in Los Angeles. The commissioners determined that the CWC's new rates would remain in place conditional on the installation of additional pumping facilities to improve the Flume system's efficiency. To meet the mandate, the company's chief engineer, William S. Post, recommended that the owners spend some $7,400 to drill additional wells powered by new, more efficient centrifugal pumps in the El Monte fields. Post warned Fletcher that if the company did not act proactively, the commissioners could restore the old rates, which would cost the company $15,000 to $20,000 in prospective income. Post argued that the company would recover the costs from the added income from the sale of the water the new wells supplied.

To forestall the commission's threat to void the new rates, Fletcher ordered Post to rush a pumping plant near the diverting dam into operation. Fletcher told Post that the commissioners were not concerned where the CWC located the plant, just that the company make an effort to improve the system and pump more water. In September 1912, Fletcher reactivated the pumping plant near the diverting dam, and by October, the company had the Chocolate Creek Plant in service; in November, the School House Plant went on line. Murray and Fletcher ramped up their CWC groundwater operations to supplement their system, avoid decreasing their water rates, meet their commercial obligations and add marketable value to their company.

After two years of operation and substantial investment in the company's infrastructure with little return, the new CWC owners hoped to sell the faltering company to the City of San Diego. In consideration of the sale, city water advisors requested detailed information on the value of the company's inventory. Among the enterprise's assets, Post estimated the value of the company's pumping plants in 1910, when Murray purchased the company, at $13,700. A civic group opposing the purchase sent investigators to check the system's condition and produced their own report for the city. Retired admiral, former custodian of San Diego's Federal Quarantine Station and now councilman H.N. Manney declared the pumping plant defective and out of date and campaigned against any deal with the CWC owners. Manney's arguments, coupled with the city's predisposition regarding the ownership of the river's waters, squelched the sale.

By November 1913, the city had rejected Murray's sales overtures, and the drought had tested the company's effectiveness as a water supplier. Post told Fletcher that the prolonged dry weather left Cuyamaca Reservoir nearly empty, the flume dry from end to end and the pumping plants functioning at reduced levels. Necessity forced Murray to expend considerable amounts on the pumping plants to maintain the system's marginal reliability and increase the system's marketability. Faced with the same water shortage, ranchers in the El Cajon Valley, in the belief that the valley's abundant underground supply would overcome the river's deficiencies, began digging wells along their riverfront lands. For the next year, the CWC and the ranchers survived almost exclusively on river groundwater.

The renewed pumping regime created a steady water supply but also created potential issues. Post worried that withdrawing so much groundwater water from the lands below the diverting dam would reduce the river's replenishment flow. He also warned Fletcher that the amount of groundwater the CWC would withdraw would decrease the supply of water for the riparian owners near Lakeside and could potentially cost the company a large amount in litigation. The warnings proved prescient.

The Lakeside Farms Mutual Water District brought suit to prevent the CWC from taking any groundwater from the Chocolate Creek beds below the company's diversion dam. The agrarians argued that drawing water from these beds would deprive the downstream riparian owners of essential water for their ranches. The CWC legal team responded with affidavits from prominent water engineers Charles Lee and J.B. Lippincott that rejected these allegations. Both Lee and Lippincott offered statements that the plant at Chocolate Creek would in no way impinge on the water supply to the lower river users. In court, CWC engineers testified that the basin was too small and the distance for the water to travel underground too great to have any influence on the Lakeside irrigators. After a day of deliberation, Judge T.L. Lewis awarded the plaintiffs $30,000 but allowed the CWC to continue drawing subsurface river water.

In 1926, prior to the sale of the CWC to the La Mesa, Lemon Grove and Spring Valley Irrigation District, the deficient natural surface flow again forced Fletcher to extract water from the riverbed lands to supplement the Flume system. Fletcher ordered new wells drilled opposite the El Monte plant and expended $36,000 to improve the El Monte pumping plant, which allowed the company to sell water at four and a half cents per one thousand gallons. The plants in the El Monte area were particularly productive. After Fletcher sold the enterprise to the Irrigation District, it continued major pumping operations in the El Monte fields until the completion of El Capitan Dam in 1934.

The river's underground water capabilities (which the irrigation district mediators conservatively appraised at $100,000) were talking points in the negotiations between the City of San Diego and the irrigation district to settle their lingering water issues in the 1930s. The city arbiters insisted that the acquisition of the Irrigation District's five hundred acres of water-bearing gravels adjacent to the El Monte Pumping Plant and the lands in the San Diego River bottoms between El Capitan Dam site and Lakeside were essential to any agreement. The groundwater lands remained active assets of the city and county landowners as the region's population expanded, particularly in the years preceding World War II.

The Helix Water District currently manages the Santee–El Monte groundwater basin, which contains approximately seventy thousand acre-feet of water. Into 2011, the Helix District operated one well in the El Monte Basin and pumped only the amount its engineers deemed could be naturally recharged. Agencies that now take groundwater from the Santee–El Monte riverbeds include the City of San Diego, the Helix Water District, the Padre Dam Municipal Water District, the Lakeside Water District and the Riverview Water District.

River Groundwater Appraisal

The town's struggle to develop the San Diego River, periodic droughts and the river's seasonal flow made river groundwater critical to the region. Before the San Diego Flume Company started transporting water from the upper river in 1888, the town's water came primarily from wells and the riverbed pumping stations that the city and private companies operated. Even with the addition of the surface water from the Southern California Mountain Water Company in 1905, the region's climatic proclivities rendered groundwater a vital source of domestic water for community residents, irrigation water for inland ranchers and farmers and water to sustain the CWC. Between 1914 and 1936, the Mission Valley aquifer was a primary source of drinking water for the city, with the river's surface flow a periodic reserve.

Increasing demand, the limitations of the regional suppliers and the uncertain supply of river surface water compelled city water experts and private entrepreneurs to tap this hidden resource. Unlike the protracted litigation to control the river, the cost of a massive river dam and the chaotic campaign to select a river dam site, pumping underground water from sources in proximity to the town's distribution system was cost efficient and technically unsophisticated. The importance of underground water was such that in the paramount water rights case between the CWC and the city, the court's 1931 decision specified that the city gained control of all the surface and underground water of the San Diego River.

Groundwater has remained an element in San Diego's water management strategy. According to the San Diego County Water Authority, in 2020 groundwater accounted for about 5 percent of the San Diego region's water supply. Considering the importance of subsurface water, it is ironic that California was the last western state to regulate groundwater with the passage of the Sustainable Groundwater Management Act in 2014. To that point, water historian Norris Hundley suggested that California's approach to groundwater management was a chaotic and environmentally destructive practice that translated into no management system at all.[11] On June 27, 2017, as per the state's mandate, the San Diego City Council formed the Groundwater Sustainability Agency to meet regional requirements.

Chapter 8

THE RIVER DAM CONTROVERSY

*One of the biggest hassles we had was trying to keep some of those idiots
from building a dam in Mission Gorge.*
—*City Councilman Fred A. Heilbron, 1919–27*

The most foolish thing that can be done is to build El Capitan Dam.
—*Ed Fletcher, 1920*

Arguing about water issues was second nature to San Diegans, and that included the San Diego River. The town citizens and civic leaders agreed that developing the river was an obvious step in the resolution of San Diego's water dilemma and agreed that the construction of a dam on the river to capture and store the river's flow, particularly during flood events, was necessary. Here the agreement faltered. While the commitment to construct a large dam on the river was universal, selecting a site engendered an unprecedented level of community division. San Diego water historian James L. Perry observed that the disagreement over the site caused years of "violent technical arguments, differences of opinion, financial maneuvers and legal battles."[1] In small-town San Diego, the debate focused as much on personalities as it did on practicality and became more a political than engineering problem.

THE SEEDS OF THE CONTROVERSY, 1870–1924

The dispute centered on whether the city should construct the dam in Mission Gorge, about eight miles east and slightly north of the city, or at El Capitan, some thirty miles east of the city. Local water advocates identified three potential dam sites in Mission Gorge, the narrow three-mile-long chaparral- and sage-covered corridor that ran between and beneath Mount Fortuna and Cowles Mountain. Similarly, engineers identified three potential El Capitan sites near the El Capitan Grande Reservation and in the board river valley below El Cajon Mountain. Proximity to the town made the Mission Gorge an early and popular option. Contemporary San Diego historian Harry Hopkins asserted that in the 1870s, local watermen had suggested placing a dam in the gorge a few miles below the Old Mission Dam, which would create a "cheap and capacious" water supply for city use.[2] But gradually, the view emerged that a large reservoir at El Capitan would create a long-term water solution for the town. As the opinions solidified, the decision to select a Mission Gorge or an El Capitan site ignited a thirty-year crusade of division and disagreement.

San Diego water entrepreneur Ed Fletcher entered the debate in 1911. Shortly after Fletcher joined with James Murray and formed the CWC in 1910, he acquired a 160-acre tract of private riverside land east of Lakeside just below El Cajon Mountain that featured a potential river dam site. Fletcher's private holding included only about half the land required for a large dam, with the other half situated on federal forest service land.[3] The innocuous purchase landed Fletcher in the center of the developing controversy.

City water experts were well aware of the importance of the El Capitan site, so when Fletcher took possession of the site, city officials quickly petitioned the Federal Land Office in Los Angeles to approve an application for an easement to allow the city to construct a dam on the adjacent land. The request occasioned a formal hearing at the Land Office in January 1916. Witnesses at the hearing included San Diego city attorney Terrence Cosgrove, Fletcher, Murray, an individual from Indian Affairs and several other experts and interested parties. Cosgrove argued that the project was public enhancement essential to the town's growth. Murray and Fletcher explained that they had expended almost $500,000 to improve the system and that the city's action would interfere with the CWC's future river developments and also impair the CWC's ability to supply the city. The Indian Affairs agent expressed his concern that the reservoir the dam

The construction of a dam in the narrow confines of nearby Mission Gorge was a popular option. *City of San Diego Office of City Clerk, Archives and Records Management.*

created would flood the land of Indian families living on the El Capitan Grande Reservation. Frank Leabert, president of the San Diego River Waters Association and the San Diego River Riparian Owners Association, argued that a dam at El Capitan would cause "irreparable damage" to the riverside users who depended on riverbed groundwater and leave the area suitable only for dry farming. On a positive note, hydrologist Charles H. Lee offered his opinion that a dam at El Capitan could conserve and deliver 26 million gallons of water daily to the city.[4]

After days of testimony, the two presiding federal officers decided that a trip to the El Capitan site to evaluate the situation was in order. A month after the trek, the board reconvened, and following several days of deliberation, the presiding federal officer cited the necessity of the project for San Diego's water future and decided for the city. Fletcher and Murray unsuccessfully appealed the board's decision. On a practical level, two parties now shared the El Capitan dam site, and neither could pursue a project without the portion the other controlled.

A dam at an El Capitan site was more expensive than a dam in Mission Gorge but created a much larger reservoir. *City of San Diego Office of City Clerk, Archives and Records Management.*

Despite the setback, Fletcher continued efforts to derail the city's plans at El Capitan. With no official capacity to do so, in 1915 Fletcher submitted a petition to President Woodrow Wilson that listed the names of fifty American Indians protesting the government's consideration to grant a portion of the reservation to the city for the construction of a dam. Fletcher disingenuously ignored the Flume's inadequate service to the reservation inhabitants and the multiple times he and Murray had attempted to place a dam and groundwater pumping plants on the reservation for the CWC's use. Then, in early 1916, when City Attorney Cosgrove submitted a motion to the Department of the Interior for supervisory power over the El Capitan land, Fletcher immediately filed a protest with the Land Office in Los Angeles and followed up with a direct appeal to Secretary of the Interior Franklin Lane. Fletcher admitted to Lane that, as a rule, municipal need determined most decisions, but in this case a decision that favored the city would be an injustice to the CWC. Fletcher maintained that the city's actions would lead to more litigation, stymie the system's development and disrupt the system's ability to supply its county and city consumers. In Fletcher's opinion, the entire affair was a matter of personal spite perpetrated by city politicians and thus was a matter of politics, not civic need. Fletcher also dubiously claimed that the CWC had the finances available and plans prepared to immediately construct a river dam.[5]

As city officials and Fletcher sparred, San Diego congressman William Kettner introduced his El Capitan Act in the House of Representatives. Because the bill involved federal land, Congress authorized a committee, which included Commissioner of Indian Affairs Cato Sells and several congressmen, to travel to San Diego and evaluate the situation. Not surprisingly, upon their return to Washington, the committee recommended the bill go forward. In February 1919, the 65th Congress approved the El Capitan Act, which granted water rights and certain lands to the City of San Diego in exchange for a resettlement agreement for the affected American Indians.

As Kettner's bill moved through Congress, Fletcher kept the dam issue before the San Diego public. Through the local media, Fletcher repeated all the arguments he had used in the Congressional Public Land Hearing in 1918. Now he also attacked the capacity of city leaders to efficiently coordinate a project of this scope and contended that the cumbersome bureaucracy inherent in municipal undertakings thwarted the city's ability to design and construct a large river dam in a timely manner. Conversely, Fletcher argued that a private corporation using non-public capital could avoid the pitfalls of city bureaucracy, gather the necessary capital, use his site in Mission Gorge, generate plans and build a large dam more expeditiously. Fletcher claimed that left in the hands of city politicians, any river dam project would become enmeshed in lengthy arguments and would need at least eight years to design, fund and open construction. In his opinion, a dam at El Capitan was a "prospect—not even a promise."[6]

While Fletcher conducted his print campaign, city policy-makers celebrated the federal government's passage of the El Capitan Act. The act officially recognized San Diego's need for additional water and gave the government's implied approval to construct a dam at El Capitan. To solidify the Congressional action, the Common Council issued a city ordinance—really a preemptive measure—directed at the CWC that acknowledged the government's approval of the El Capitan condemnation and then passed a city resolution that directed City Attorney Higgins to take all legal steps to "protect and safeguard the rights and interests" Congress had granted the city.[7] The city's predilection for a dam at El Capitan, however, did not quell the public advocacy for a gorge dam.

Everyone in San Diego, it seemed, had an opinion. Fletcher wanted a multiple-arch dam on land he owned in Mission Gorge. John Spreckels, who disliked Fletcher, opposed any plan Fletcher supported and labeled Fletcher anti-city and profit-minded. For once, Fletcher agreed with his rival Hiram Savage about placing a dam in the gorge, but each wanted a different type of dam at a different location. Different mayors favored different sites. The Common Council members divided over the location issue, and their division boiled over into an argument regarding the ability of City Water Manager Savage to develop a suitable municipal water plan. The El Capitan Grande Indians voiced a preference for a gorge dam, but their voices were deemed inconsequential and ignored. Even the usually monolithic chamber split over the issue.

City hall was not immune to the debate. In September 1920, City Water Commissioners Horace Aughe and Charles Sumner attempted to derail the growing El Capitan movement with a scheme to draw $600,000 of city money away from the El Capitan fund. Their scheme centered on the construction of another water conduit on Dulzura Creek. The Dulzura Conduit, a fourteen-mile-long open aqueduct that conveyed water between Barrett Reservoir and Lower Otay Reservoir, was already in place. Fred Heilbron and some of his council compatriots recognized the commissioners' new conduit plan as a piece of political subterfuge and used the moment to repeat the call for "El Capitan First." They framed the construction of an El Capitan dam as the "most important project today facing the citizens of San Diego" and declared that the city would construct El Capitan despite the resistance of the principal naysayers Murray and Fletcher. Frederick Sterns, attorney for the San Diego Consolidated Gas & Electric Company and a personal friend of Fletcher's, warned the oppositional councilmen that the city faced years of litigation before an El Capitan project would go forward. Councilman Donald Stewart answered through the *San Diego Union* with a demonstrative, "Let them start their litigation, we are loaded for bear."[8] The proposal failed, but the bitterness grew.

The lack of progress on such a political issue motivated a response from the City Water commissioners in April 1921. The commissioners issued a report to Mayor John Bacon and the council that rebuked city officials for choosing sides based on personal preference rather than civic need and urged city leaders to end the lingering controversy, acquire the rights to the river and develop the river. They conceded that it was a difficult and convoluted undertaking and called for an atmosphere of "perfect harmony and mutual confidence" to complete the "delicate and difficult task."[9] The commission report mirrored the civic atmosphere. It was not a lack of effort but a lack of consensus that stymied progress.

Left: Local businessman John D. Spreckels often used his wealth and political power to influence San Diego water policy. *City of San Diego Water Department Archive.*

Below: Mayor John L. Bacon fought to construct a dam at the site City Engineer Hiram Savage favored in Mission Gorge. *San Diego History Center.*

Fletcher opportunistically followed the Water Commission report with his own unsolicited assessment that June. Again through the friendly local media, Fletcher argued to Mayor Bacon that the quickest way to improve the city's water status was to build a gorge dam, preferably on his site; build his proposed Fletcher Dam on the upper river; and authorize the city to purchase the CWC. Fletcher ignored any suggestion of an El Capitan project.

City water managers ignored Fletcher's self-serving suggestions and decided to consult a third-party expert. Through City Attorney Higgins, the council solicited the advice of multiple-arch dam expert John Eastwood. Given Fletcher's patronage of Eastwood (Eastwood had constructed four of his arched dams in San Diego County in 1917 and 1918), the city's selection of Eastwood was an intriguing move. Nevertheless, Eastwood investigated the two Mission Gorge sites and two sites at El Capitan and, as a gesture to Fletcher, visited the reservoir site Fletcher proposed above the CWC diversion dam. In the report Eastwood issued to Mayor Bacon and the Common Council in July 1921, he discounted Savage's gorge site and one of the El Capitan sites as unsatisfactory and implied that the excessive cost of building a dam at any El Capitan location made that project unacceptable. Not surprisingly, Eastwood advocated a 230-foot dam at Fletcher's gorge site in combination with another large dam at the Fletcher site on the upper river. He also suggested the city purchase the CWC. Fletcher was delighted—El Capitan supporters were unmoved.

Frustrated with the civic division, in January 1922 Mayor Bacon issued a public appeal for unity. In the statement, he called on all citizens to put aside their differences, consider all options with an open mind—no matter who presented them—and work together. This was a community issue, not a personal issue. Bacon asked all concerned to apply the San Diego spirit, learn the facts, make educated decisions and come together as a community. Ever the politician, Bacon then took the opportunity to praise City Hydraulic Engineer Hiram Savage, the city's strong-willed chief hydrologist. After Savage graduated from the School of Engineering at Dartmouth College, he began his professional career in San Diego in 1891, worked with the United States Reclamation Service and then returned to become San Diego's lead water engineer in 1916. Bacon urged citizens to rely on Savage's integrity and professional ability and then tasked Savage to prepare a comprehensive water plan for the city.

In November 1922, Savage presented his plan. Savage's report opened with a warning that at the present pace of consumption, the city would need increased reservoir storage by 1926 or suffer the consequences of severe water deprivation. Savage prepared a detailed graphic that compared the unit cost for distributing 1 million gallons of water per day from the dams at Mission Gorge and El Capitan and estimated the construction costs for each dam. As expected, Savage concluded that a dam at the site he favored in Mission Gorge was the most cost-efficient choice. He reasoned that a dam there required a shorter conveyance system, the location facilitated an efficient gravity-flow system to the city distribution plant and, if desired, the city could easily heighten any dam constructed in the narrow confines of the gorge. Savage was a polarizing figure in San Diego's water landscape, so naturally his supporters applauded the plan and his opponents scoffed.

The Common Council fired Hiram Savage in 1923 and then rehired him in 1928. *City of San Diego Water Department Archive.*

The Savage Report unintentionally presented the oppositional members of the Common Council with an opening to challenge Savage. Shortly after Savage's plan went public, these dissident members of the Common Council tasked the two current members of the City Water Commission, Frederick M. White and Charles T. Chandler, to examine Savage's plan and offer alternatives. The openly anti-Savage duo summarily rejected the majority of the engineer's conclusions. The commissioners took umbrage at his suggestion of a gorge dam and chided Savage for dismissing the possibility of purchasing the CWC and pursuing the construction of Sutherland Dam, a project he openly opposed. The politically motivated commissioners then moved from technical issues and generically blamed the city's current water malaise on Savage's (although unidentified) mistakes.

The commissioners' remarks outraged Mayor Bacon, an outspoken Savage and gorge supporter. Bacon read the commission report, summarily fired the authors and sponsored a successful ballot issue to disband the Water Commission. Fletcher responded with an attack on Bacon for discharging and disgracing two of the town's most public-spirited men with the intention of creating a new agency that would do the mayor's bidding.

Despite the mayor's vengeance, the anti-Savage faction used the report as an opportunity to attack Savage. Local political cartoonists had a field day. The *San Diego Sun* mocked Savage as a missionary begging for city tax dollars

Savage was a controversial and polarizing figure in San Diego water politics. *City of San Diego Water Department Archive.*

to support a questionable political scheme while holding a sign warning of the "Drought Bugaboo." Another evinced a scene at a carnival with a barker summoning people to see the "Mission Gorge Savage" who mysteriously promised wonders. Savage's opponents perceived him as dogmatically inflexible and unwilling to compromise his programs for the good of the city.

The Savage Report and the oppositional reaction inflamed the dam site battle. Gorge supporters rehashed all the old arguments for Mission Gorge and asked why the city would expend $5 million to $7 million to build El Capitan when a gorge dam was a more economical option at $2.5 million. Their dam expert, City Consulting Engineer Thomas H. King, explained that the gorge's narrow walled configuration and the presence of a solid bedrock foundation could support a modest, less expensive concrete gravity dam, while El Capitan required a massive, costly filled structure. A gorge reservoir also required a much shorter, less costly water delivery system than did remote El Capitan. The gorge advocates pointed out that the lands at the gorge sites were readily available as private land, while federal property disputes would complicate any El Capitan project.

The El Capitan backers responded in kind. They argued that a gorge reservoir would create a shallow reservoir susceptible to excessive evaporation and that the reservoir would flood all of Santee and much of Lakeside and inundate about one-third of the El Cajon Valley and destroy valuable farm and ranch lands. They also expressed health concerns about taking tainted water from a reservoir that submerged ranch and dairy lands and old septic tanks in El Cajon, Santee and Lakeside. The pro–El Capitan advocates explained that the large reservoir at El Capitan had the capacity to hold enough water to truly impact the city supply, store any future imported water and offer a more efficient flood control than any small gorge structure.

The members of the chamber of commerce addressed the issue and whole-heartedly agreed on the development of the San Diego River. There the agreement ended. The matter split the generally monolithic organization. Some members favored Fletcher's gorge site, others endorsed

Savage's choice, while still others favored El Capitan. The divided body even pondered Fletcher's suggestion of constructing Fletcher Dam on the upper river in combination with a gorge dam. The only point of consensus was to solicit another third-party professional.

The oppositional environment within the city broadened and intensified the debate, further fragmented the already divided forces, encouraged options rather than solutions and hindered substantive progress. A defining moment came when the council fired Savage in June 1923. Savage's dismissal involved personal, philosophical and political differences. As a professionally trained and experienced engineer, Savage resented what he considered interference from amateurs, and after months of disagreement the council members orchestrated Savage's removal. The day after the council discharged Savage, City Manager Fred Rhodes, who reported directly to the council, issued an official statement arguing that Savage was fired because he ignored Rhodes's orders and questioned his authority and because he was dissatisfied with Savage's overall management of city water projects. Savage's supporters decried the political nature of the firing.

In an attempt to bring calm and clarity to the citywide confusion, in August 1923 the Common Council hired imminent eastern water engineer Dr. John R. Freeman to survey and comment on the county's water resources. Freeman roamed the countryside for almost nine months as he gathered information and evaluated possibilities. He completed his investigations and presented the findings at a much-anticipated and crowded Common Council meeting in May 1924. In his presentation, Freeman denounced the use of Fletcher's multi-arch dams in general and specifically rejected a dam at Fletcher's gorge site. Freeman believed that Savage's gorge site was superior in terms of water storage capacity and construction cost and recommended the construction of a concrete gravity dam there. Freeman's conclusions were at variance with the opinions of most of the council members, particularly El Capitan supporter Councilman Heilbron. Heilbron constantly interrupted Freeman's presentation and bombarded the engineer with questions and criticisms. The meeting adjourned with some professional feelings hurt and with more questions than answers. As had the Savage Report and Fletcher's unsolicited comments, rather than mitigating the situation Freeman's suggestions fueled the divisive atmosphere.[10]

The chamber Water Committee followed Freeman's report with its compromise plan. The committee members prefaced their proposal with a plea for citizens and leaders to put aside their conflicting opinions for the public good and for the members of the Common Council to cease indulging in endless debate and make a sincere effort to end the internecine contention. The politically savvy members publicly preached civic accommodation but internally worried that addressing the water-related circumstances would lead to expensive and lengthy litigation, heated negotiations and probably adversely affect the development of the San Diego River. Four months after Freeman presented his ideas, the committee members unveiled their water scheme.

The chamber's plan was truly an attempt at compromise. The proposal included elements of virtually every water proposition presented over the past decade. The plan called for the city to purchase the CWC, negotiate a river water-sharing agreement with the La Mesa, Lemon Grove and Spring Valley Irrigation District and, omitting any details, develop the river. The chamber leadership also suggested that the Common Council contract with an unbiased third-party engineer, perhaps one from the federal government, to gain new insights into the dispute. The chamber's plan was a desperate entreaty to reunite the community, somehow tap the river and get water flowing and grow the city. Unfortunately, the chamber's amalgamated program of accommodation pleased few, antagonized many and failed to overcome the discord.

Chamber member and councilman Fred Heilbron responded to the chamber's compromise plan with a counterproposal. The tall, lanky ex-plumber turned lawyer arrived in San Diego in 1888, the same year as Ed Fletcher, and won a council seat in 1919 running on a water improvement platform. In his plan, and contrary to his friend Fletcher, Heilbron contended that El Capitan was the key to the San Diego River. He believed that a dam there would control "every drop of water in the river" and render a gorge dam unnecessary. Heilbron's chamber and civic supporters argued that it was not in the city's best interest to place a "stop-gap dam" in the gorge and wait twenty years to develop a significant structure at El Capitan. He reminded all parties that while Congress had approved the land grant to the El Capitan site through the 1919 El Capitan Act, the city would forfeit all those rights unless it took action by December 22, 1924. As to the circumstance of relocating the Native Americans on the El Capitan Grande Reservation, Heilbron and his backers thought that the city should provide reasonable compensation to the dispossessed bands, but that it was the duty of the Interior Department, not the city, to deal with that issue. The Heilbron faction also maintained that it was incumbent that the city condemn the El Capitan lands while they were in private ownership. If the El Capitan lands passed to a municipality or a water district, the situation would become infinitely more complicated.[11] Ironically, the same water issues that brought Helibron and Fletcher together as friends eventually pulled them apart.

Frustrated with the inaction, the council voted unanimously to order City Attorney Higgins to prepare and present the San Diego Superior Court with condemnation papers for the Mission Gorge and El Capitan sites. The condemnation papers stated that the city would offer a fair price for the land and indicated that the city contemplated constructing dams at both sites. The council, in a rare display of unanimity and perhaps in the hope of settling the dam site issue, justified the action as an emergency measure to protect the city's interests. The condemnation suit lingered in the court system until 1927, when the California Appellate Court ruled that the city at that time did not have the right to acquire title to the sites through eminent domain and closed the proceedings.

SEEKING A SOLUTION, 1924–1934

By late 1924, the controversy had reached a tipping point. After all the arguments, editorials and opinions, the members of the Common Council finally accepted that the level of public and political division forestalled a mediated resolution and called for a special election. The key proposition on the November 18, 1924 ballot requested a $4.5 million bond for necessary municipal water improvements, the purchase of the required lands and rights of way, the installation of associated distribution pipelines, the fabrication of a water filtration plant and the construction of an arched, gravity masonry dam at El Capitan site no. 2 on the San Diego River. The decision now rested with the city voters.

By this point, the issue had divided the community into three camps: the citizens who supported either the gorge or El Capitan and those who just wanted the matter settled. Citizen committees on both sides launched public informational meetings, preached their respective views and predicted victory. The opponents gathered in school auditoriums, churches, community centers and social clubs, where the rhetoric often became inflamed and the arguments heated. City Auditor H.L. Moody, a frequent spokesman on the city tour, labeled the gorge people as "traitors to the city interest" who had long "throttled and thwarted" the city. Moody singled out Ed Fletcher for his opposition and called it ironic that the money the people of San Diego paid the CWC for water was used to stifle the El Capitan project.[12]

Mayor Bacon lashed out at El Capitan supporters Spreckels and Heilbron as only interested in the personal profit they would garner from a contract to construct the million-dollar pipeline running from El Capitan Reservoir to the city. Each side offered free tours out to the gorge and El Capitan dam sites to lecture citizens on the comparative advantages of each and urged the public to make an informed decision.

To gain an advantage, the El Capitan faction also produced a silent movie. Frank Belcher, the president of the First National Bank, authorized Higgins and City Manager Rhodes to contact a small production company to create a film contrasting the two sites. Of course, the film featured the limitations of the gorge and the perfect locale at El Capitan. The film concluded with the image of a huge, pristine lake and a caption illustrating what El Capitan would look like once it filled with pure mountain water. The movie screened in every local theater the week before the election.

Amazingly, while the sides sparred and the election approached, alternative water plans continued to appear. Only months before the election, the Common Council requested Rhodes write a synopsis of the water studies of Mayor Bacon's Water Committee and the chamber compromise plan. Another faction proposed a desperation plan that called for a dam at Gorge site no. 2, the purchase of the Gorge no. 3 site and any lands the reservoir would flood and the acquisition of water-bearing lands on the San Dieguito River. Hydraulic Engineer Thomas H. King, a former engineer for the CWC, presented a plan that was largely a modification of the plan Fred Rhodes had earlier offered the council. John F. Covert, former engineer for the Sweetwater Water Company and then chief engineer for a San Diego construction company, put forward a modification of the Savage and King Plans with dam at Mission Gorge no. 2, with structures at El Capitan and San Vincente to follow. Both King and Covert included the potential use of El Capitan Reservoir as a storage facility for Colorado River water.

Significantly, Savage and Heilbron recognized the potential of bringing water from a source outside the county and pressed city officials to investigate the concept. In 1926, the city actuated a filing for Colorado River water. However, engineering and legal complexities, financial obligations and philosophical differences, mainly the assumption that the city's current water resources, including the development of the San Diego River, were sufficient for the near future, blunted the movement. Savage and his like-minded associates recognized that San Diego's increasing population would inevitably overwhelm the county's available resources, but the notion of imported water was simply premature.

The sides argued, the candidates debated and the divided city braced for Election Day. The community campaigning culminated with a much-anticipated public debate on the eve of the election in a packed Spreckels' Theater, the lavish Baroque-style building Spreckels constructed in 1912. Mayor Bacon represented the gorge side, while Moody and Higgins spoke for the El Capitan backers. Had the council not fired Savage, Bacon's friend and staunch gorge supporter, the engineer would have undoubtedly been at Bacon's side on the stage. Moderator Fred Mitchell introduced the participants, and the audience response quickly made it clear that this was an El Capitan crowd. The evening morphed from a debate into a rally for El Capitan. Higgins opened with a "logical and thoughtful analysis" of the situation, presented the legal process the city used to gain the river and explained why he believed El Capitan was the best option to develop the river. Mayor Bacon retorted that El Capitan was a "$4,500,000 bet" that rested on the uncertain outcome of a pending Supreme Court decision. Bacon, a former civil engineer turned politician, introduced the only new issue when he argued that engineers could not locate the bedrock at El Capitan with any certainty, which raised serious safety concerns. Moody responded with information from the Freeman Report that countered Bacon's accusations. From that point, the evening lapsed into a reiteration of past arguments, while hecklers interrupted the speakers with catcalls and taunts, most often the call to "Build El Capitan Now." The pro-Fletcher *San Diego Sun* pointed out that Bacon won considerable applause as he fought a single-handed battle against two opponents before an assemblage that clearly had no sympathy with his position.[13]

The November election also included a mayoral race. The candidate and the incumbent recognized the importance of addressing the community's water circumstance. The challenger, businessman Walter W. Austin, faced incumbent John Bacon. Bacon stood on his record as a water advocate. Austin recalled that in the last decade, voters had approved more than $8 million for water development, so he mildly attacked Bacon for his lack of accomplishments and likewise ran on a water improvement platform and hoped that his support of El Capitan would carry him to victory.

Almost 25,000 voters marched to the polls for the November 18 referendum. The evening of the election, Higgins had a movie screen attached on the building across from city hall to project the updated vote count as volunteers telephoned in the results. The voters elected Austin mayor and overwhelmingly approved the El Capitan bond issue 18,131 to 6,624. The pro-gorge faction finally expressed signs of resignation. The citizen committee that opposed El Capitan accepted the plebiscite, and Fletcher publicly acknowledged the voters' sentiment for El Capitan, while also expressing his determination to continue his personal and legal crusade.

After years of community division, it appeared that the election and mutual exhaustion marked the end in the dam site affair. But the divide was too deep and the sides too polarized. The election produced a result, not a solution. It appeared that San Diego voters did not trust their own judgment. The electorate passed the measure, but it took ten more years, two more civic votes and the loss of billions of gallons of river water into the sea before the townspeople settled the issue.

Between 1924 and 1928, San Diego's water development entered a stage of relative inactivity. Desperate to remedy the city's stagnating water circumstances, the city fathers turned to the deposed Savage. Following his dismissal from city service in 1923, Savage undertook a series of international tours and served as a consulting engineer on several U.S. Reclamation Service projects. Even in his absence the council believed that he was the most qualified person to resuscitate the town's water prospects. After a five-year hiatus, the newly elected Common Council rehired Savage in July 1928. With a four-to-one vote (the lone dissenter being Savage's longtime nemesis, E.H. Dowell), the council presented him with a five-year $10,000-per-year contract. Having experienced the fickle nature of San Diego water politics, Savage accepted on the condition that the council guarantee that he would be free from political interference. The councilmen concurred, and Savage sailed from Europe within the week. The editor of the *San Diego Union* praised the action, while those of the *San Diego Sun* and the *San Diego Labor Leader* decried the decision and asked, "Why Savage?" Typical of the strong-minded engineer, before entering San Diego city limits, Savage departed the train at the stop in backcountry Campo, organized transportation and motored north to the Sutherland Dam site, where he summarily canceled work on the multiple-arch endeavor he had long opposed.

The Common Council immediately assigned Savage a new title and new tasks. As the city hydraulic engineer in charge of the Municipal Bureau of Water Development, Savage served at the pleasure of the council, not the city manager. Among his many new duties, the council ordered him to prepare a comprehensive city water strategy that included the development of the San Diego River. Savage ignored the oppositional assaults, drew on his expertise and knowledge of the county's water landscape and compiled his second (the first in 1922) holistic municipal water development program.

Savage presented his plan, "Sources of Additional Water Supply," to Mayor Harry C. Clark and the Common Council in September 1928. In the plan, Savage reiterated the generic need for a stable municipal water supply program, explained how the city's increasing water consumption affected future water needs and addressed the issues of overdrawing on the Cottonwood and Otay systems and over-pumping the subsurface river groundwater in Lakeside, Riverview and Mission Valley. All these factors made developing the San Diego River a necessity. In an effort to appear unbiased, and without abandoning his preference for a gorge dam, Savage conceded that the river contained several workable flood runoff catchment locations on the upper and lower river, which could serve as storage reservoirs. But in Savage's mind, at this point, the location of a new river dam was secondary to establishing a comprehensive municipal water development plan. Like all preceding water plans, Savage's proposal quickly entered the public and political gristmill.

The year was 1928, but it felt like 1924. Unable to implement a city water agenda, the council called on the community to return to the polls in the summer of 1931. Both sides ramped up their public media campaigns. They launched newspaper broadsides and issued pamphlets, organized public informational events and presented slide programs to promote their respective views. The opponents faced off in civic clubs and at PTA meetings, in labor union halls and in churches. The El Capitan faction argued how the larger reservoir would serve the future needs of the city and not flood valuable farmlands. The gorge people argued that Savage's long-standing advocacy of a gorge dam prevented him from ever building a dam at El Capitan and pitched cheaper water with a quicker construction time on land the city already owned. Fletcher, no longer aligned with a water agency, assailed El Capitan, disparaged Savage's gorge site choice and touted his gorge location.

Taking a wrinkle from the 1924 campaign, the chamber leaders sponsored the production of a motion picture. They presented a talkie at local theaters the week preceding the vote that featured Savage and chamber president Hal Hotchkiss at the edge of Chollas Reservoir discussing San Diego's water future, with the sound of workmen repairing a leaky pipe in the background. Mayor Clark called the movie a piece of "heavy ammunition" in the fight to pass the water bond. The *Union* declared it the first recorded voice of any San Diegan.[14]

With election looming, the chamber of commerce orchestrated a public information forum in late 1930. A chamber committee invited a cross-section of water professionals, amateur engineers, attorneys and laymen to

The El Capitan supporters screened the town's first "talkie" movie to promote their agenda in the 1929 water bond election. *From* San Diego Magazine *(1929).*

offer opinions. The anticipated presentations of Savage, King and Fletcher piqued the public interest.

Savage appeared before the chamber directors in December. He recommended that the city sponsor an election allowing the city to transfer appropriations from the Chollas Heights and the Sutherland projects to fund preliminary dam designs and then construct a masonry dam across the San Diego River in Mission Gorge at site no. 2. Water engineer Thomas King followed Savage in early January 1931. King called the development of the San Diego River the most important matter the city faced and admonished the chamber to "apply their business common sense" to "get the most for their money" and build a dam at El Capitan.[15] In February, Fletcher presented his views. As expected, the loquacious Fletcher attacked any scheme at El Capitan and any plan in Mission Gorge that did not include his property. In supporting his site, Fletcher pointed to the expense of an El Capitan dam and exhorted the city, which was operating from the "position of a man with a champagne appetite and a beer pocketbook," to "live within its means" and construct his gorge dam. In typical Fletcher fashion, he believed that any faction that pressed for the construction of a major dam on the river other than the gorge was simply trying to "stampede the voters" into an unnecessary action.[16] The chamber had snubbed John Freeman, but the engineer nevertheless offered his unsolicited views in March 1931. Freeman reiterated his 1924 recommendations, stating that in his opinion Savage's gorge dam offered the most water for the least expense, but again obliquely recognized the potential of El Capitan.

In a show of civic responsibility, the chamber also initiated a city-wide multimedia campaign to turn out the vote. The group authorized city publicity agents to produce and distribute posters, placards for autos and window displays encouraging voter participation. On Election Day, city workers organized local Boy Scout troops to canvas the town block by block, reminding citizens to get out and vote.

City voters gathered on August 11, 1931, and by a mere 879 votes defeated a proposition to construct a gorge dam, but they did not approve a dam at El Capitan either. The community continued to function in a state of divisiveness, which exacerbated the civic debate and proved counterproductive in advancing the town's water circumstances. The opponents understood the need to dispense with the rancor, bitterness and destructive criticism, to ignore the personality conflicts and proceed as a united citizenry, but the polarity of their respective positions stifled conciliation.

With the site issue unresolved and the close vote in the last election in mind, the Common Council called for another special election in December 1931. This time, the results were decisive. More than 80 percent of the electorate reaffirmed the 1924 decision to construct a dam at El Capitan.

The winners used the election as a directive to push the El Capitan project and depose Savage. In their anti-Savage tracts, Patrick O'Rourke, the chairman of the El Capitan Committee, demanded the city hire an "opened minded" engineer who would embrace the El Capitan project. The *Herald* published a cartoon showing the citizens of San Diego offering Savage a ticket back to Cairo, Egypt; harped that Savage was now finished in San Diego; and featured an editorial telling its readers that the city did not have a water problem—it had a Savage problem. But the afterglow of victory turned into frustration when the newly renamed City Council voted three to two to retain Savage as the city water chief. The editor of the *San Diego Sun* summarized the city's mood when he opined that San Diegans were tired of the dispute over Savage, weighted down with the Mission Gorge–El Capitan fight, and that the community just wanted public accord, a river project completed and the water flowing.

With the river secured and the 1931 plebiscite reconfirming the dam site, city officials set the El Capitan project into motion. Savage accepted the decision of the voters and ordered the city engineering force to create an operating budget, draft designs and secure the land and the necessary right of ways. Significantly, Fletcher relinquished his El Capitan properties to the city in early 1932.

Between 1920 and 1930, as San Diego added almost seventy-four thousand residents, city water experts pondered how to manage a static water supply to sate the needs of the town's increasing population. But with the site controversy settled and El Capitan on the horizon, most San Diegans were satisfied with the direction of the town's water future.

Chapter 9

THE RIGHT TO RULE THE RIVER

*Supplying the city with water is a measure
fraught with the weightiest and vital public interest.
—Resolution, San Diego Chamber of Commerce, 1894*

San Diego historian William Wright noted that in the first decades of the twentieth century, the attempts of San Diegans to master the San Diego River supplied more civic agitation than beneficial water. In Wright's words, the struggle to control the river "inspired argument, dispute, contradiction, bitterness, political wrangling, deception, litigation, and internecine warfare."[1]

AN OPINION AND A PUEBLO RIGHT

The issue of who would manage the river took on a new urgency when Murray and Fletcher launched the Cuyamaca Water Company in 1910. Fletcher and Murray saw the CWC as a business opportunity and chafed at the idea that the city would curtail their established water operation. City leaders operated under the implicit assumption that the city possessed the right to all the waters of the river and saw the CWC's actions as a threat to a municipal resource. The control of the river cast meaningful implications. For the city, managing the river meant water stability and municipal expansion.

For the CWC, the river water held the key to the company's business future. The ensuing skirmishes between the city and the CWC established the tone of contention and set the strategic legal benchmarks that the two rivals employed over the next fifteen years. Both understood that there could be only one master of the river.

In an attempt to solidify the city's governance of the river, in 1913 city officials solicited legal views on the matter. The results were mixed. Local magistrate W.T. McNealy responded that in his opinion the city indeed possessed the prior and paramount right to the river waters, while City Attorney W.R. Andrews, who later served as judge in the first river court case, asserted that he believed the city had no such prerogative. Pro-growth Mayor Charles O'Neil ignored his city attorney and in a message to the Common Council in May 1913 urged city representatives to act immediately and protect the town's rights to the river waters. Following O'Neil's declaration, Andrews issued a written protest and resigned his office. Within days of Andrews's departure, the Common Council met and appointed local lawyer and water advocate Terence B. Cosgrove the new city attorney and assigned him his first official task.

In November 1913, the Common Council via a city resolution directed Cosgrove to investigate and offer his insights on the rights of the City of San Diego relating to the San Diego River. In the eyes of the municipality, the management of the river was a public trust issue, and the council wanted a clear message in that regard. City leaders sought exclusive control of the river and intended to establish that right. To that end, the council authorized the creation of a document that protected the city's interest and demonstrated its claim to the river. As Cosgrove approached his assignment, he was undoubtedly aware of the Water Commission Act of 1913, a bill designed to regulate and license the diversion of the state's surface water and groundwater, being debated in the state legislature. In January 1914, Cosgrove presented "An Opinion on the Rights of the City of San Diego to the Waters of the San Diego River" to the Common Council.

To create historic perspective, Cosgrove systematically researched Spanish and Mexican colonial historical records, documents and laws, as well as pertinent court decisions. Cosgrove applied the concept of judicial notice, which allowed the researcher to use materials experts had authoritatively attested as authentic in his inquiry. Still, the bulk of this evidence on the status of the pueblo of San Diego, its relationship to community water resources and the concept that a grant from the king of Spain formed the basis for the city's claim was inferential.

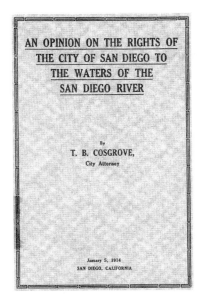

AN OPINION ON THE RIGHTS OF
THE CITY OF SAN DIEGO TO
THE WATERS OF THE
SAN DIEGO RIVER

By
T. B. COSGROVE,
City Attorney

January 5, 1914
SAN DIEGO, CALIFORNIA

City Attorney Terence Cosgrove penned the "Opinion of 1914," which codified the city's right to the San Diego River. *Author's collection.*

From his research, Cosgrove asserted that when the Spanish administrators organized the pueblo of San Diego in 1769, they intended for the religious and military branches and the mission and the presidio to function separately. The crux of the contention declared that the colonial laws, via royal grants, guaranteed the pueblo the prerogative to hold water rights for the use of the citizens, and that prerogative superseded those of the mission and the presidio. While the government did not reference specific water grants for a pueblo, the capacity to use water was understood as a natural right for inhabitants on all pueblo lands. This status continued under the Mexican government in 1821 and passed to the United States under the Treaty of Guadalupe-Hidalgo, where it was transferred to the new American town.

As to the question of adverse possession, Cosgrove and his city legal colleagues reasoned that because the urban inhabitants had continuously used the river waters and retained title to the land and water, any property (water) held by a town considered the successor to a pueblo could not be forfeited with the passage of time. Cosgrove concluded that the City of San Diego had the prior and paramount right to use the river waters for the general public and for all municipal purposes.[2]

Cosgrove buttressed his argument with precedents from relevant legal decisions. He specifically referenced the findings from *Lux v. Haggin* in 1886 and the 1895 *Vernon Irrigation Company v. The City of Los Angeles* case wherein the court declared that any stream flowing through public land was a part of the title of that land. Cosgrove relied heavily on the legal stratagem Los Angeles attorney John Godfrey contrived in *Feliz v. The City of Los Angeles* in 1881, where the City of Los Angeles sought control of the Los Angeles River. Godfrey successfully argued that no entity could interfere with the right of the city to take water from any point on the river at its convenience. This line of reasoning fostered the pueblo rights water theory.

The pueblo rights concept essentially allowed a qualifying community to claim all the water required for municipal development regardless of other competing user claims. Water historian Norris Hundley suggested that Godfrey manufactured a theory that the legal community ultimately accepted as a legitimate doctrine. In Hundley's estimation, the theory ran counter to the basic principles of appropriation doctrine and riparian rights, California's accepted water rights criterion. Hundley noted that the legal community accepted the theory because it stressed the rights of the community over the individual, a particularly attractive political philosophy in the waning years of the Progressive movement in California.[3] Water rights expert Wells Hutchins likewise thought that the pueblo rights theory rested on a series of judicial notice presumptions and said the treatment of the Spanish and Mexican laws in the California cases was based on a very narrow foundation. Hutchins also supported the adverse possession, saying that the pueblo theory supplanted the rights of private interests that had exercised beneficial use to consumers for generations.[4] Contrived or not, Cosgrove saw the theory as his golden bullet.

The public response to Cosgrove's "Opinion" was remarkably subdued. Cosgrove later admitted that on the day the piece went public, citizens treated it like a routine news item. The *San Diego Sun* wrote that Cosgrove declared in thirty typewritten pages filled with flowery phrases that the city had first call on the river water. The *Sun* downplayed the implications of the document and instead noted how Cosgrove ignored using confusing legal terms and put some human nature into his writing. The same day, the *San Diego Union* relegated the news to page five and then blandly reiterated the next day that the "Oldest Records Show City's Right to San Diego River." Both newspapers filled more space explaining Cosgrove's research and the use of historical records than editorializing the content of the document. In his annual message to the city on January 6, the day after the city released the "Opinion," Mayor Charles O'Neil included a recommendation to secure the El Capitan dam site but made no mention of the document.[5]

Fletcher and Murray had a very different response. The well-spoken and popular Fletcher, while the minority partner, was the public spokesman for the CWC and sensed the implicit threat the "Opinion" presented to their business. Fletcher immediately responded with interviews in sympathetic newspapers and announced that he was ready to "go on the war path." Fletcher asserted that Cosgrove authored the missive for the "sole purpose of annoying, vexing, and harassing" and hindering the development of the CWC. Respective headlines supporting the CWC declared that the owners were willing to "Fight for River Water Rights" and that the "Rights of City to Water a Joke." Fletcher pointed out that the San Diego Flume

Company and the CWC had taken water for the benefit of citizens for the past thirty years and questioned why the city now decided to announce a claim to the river.[6] Through the friendly *San Diego Sun*, Fletcher argued that the "Opinion" was the city's first indication that the municipality intended to claim sole possession of the river. Fletcher asked why had public officials waited until 1914 to initiate any action and observed, not coincidentally, that the "Opinion" appeared at the very moment the CWC directors considered projects to dam the river and institute other upper river improvements. Fletcher ignored the company's checkered service record, touted its contribution to local water development and argued that the improvements to the CWC would bring more water to the city and aid the city's growth. Fletcher questioned the city's motives to hinder a private utility that had served the community for decades. Fletcher made it clear that despite the city's stance, the CWC owners planned to continue to commercialize river water and improve the system.

Fletcher fumed and the city acted. The Common Council served notice of the municipality's paramount right to the river through a city resolution in May 1914. The document stated that because "certain persons, individuals and companies" made and contemplated further development of the San Diego River, the council and the city's Board of Water Commissioners felt compelled to reassert the city's prior right to the river. While the council's statement, an obvious reference to Fletcher and the CWC, was more procedural than legal, it clearly stated the city's position.

Using the "Opinion" as a civic manifesto, city bureaucrats unveiled their proactive river strategy and declared the city's public intent to gain exclusive control of the river. The city's aggressive change in strategy was timely. In City Attorney Shelley Higgins's words, the city had been "sleeping" on those river rights far too long and needed to assert its hegemony over the river.[7] In the spring of 1914, the Common Council passed a city resolution, really a public policy statement, that emphasized that any conversations or agreements between the city and the CWC could not be construed in any way to interfere with the city's rights to the river. Then, in March, it issued another resolution, which stated that purchasing water from the CWC did not represent any concession of the city's claim to the river. City policy-makers publicly and clearly declared their stance regarding individuals or groups that took or intended to take river water for business purposes. The control of the river was at stake, and public administrators used the "Opinion" to establish a blueprint of evidential documentation to defend against the anticipated litigation.

Given the success of the pueblo rights theory in Los Angeles, Cosgrove believed that the application of the concept in San Diego was tactically sound. The town's Spanish and Mexican heritage and the location of the river within the city limits certainly mirrored the particulars of the *Vernon* and *Feliz* cases. With this in mind, the San Diego legal contingent crafted an argument they believed proved San Diego was the successor to the original pueblo of San Diego that the Spanish established in 1769. The pueblo rights theory also extricated the city from a potentially troublesome circumstance where the San Diego legal team would have negotiated the river rights from a weaker position based on California's traditional riparian and appropriative rights concepts. Cosgrove's "Opinion" was a seminal document that staked a municipal claim to the underdeveloped river and provided the foundations for the city's legal strategy.

THE CONGRESSIONAL HEARING OF 1918

Representatives of the city and the CWC took the opportunity to present their respective positions on river rights in January 1918, when the House of Representatives Committee on Public Lands agreed to deliberate Congressman William Kettner's pending legislation on the conservation of water in San Diego. Kettner, recently elected on a platform centered on harbor improvements, requested the hearing as a platform to leverage the city's condemnation proceedings on the dam site lands on the El Capitan Grande Indian Reservation. City officials saw the hearing as an occasion to solidify popular and political support for their river agenda. Fletcher saw the hearing as an opportunity to prove that the city's agenda was more sinister than publicly professed and to persuade the committee and the community that the city's actions were simply a maneuver to gain control of the CWC and secure the El Capitan dam site. Fletcher also viewed the hearing as an opening to publicly attack the city's pueblo rights theory. Given the inevitability of future courtroom clashes, both parties anticipated the hearing as a preliminary opportunity to craft their legal arguments and hone respective strategies.

The hearing essentially pitted City Attorney Cosgrove against one of the town's prominent citizens and most successful water and real estate entrepreneurs, Ed Fletcher. Other individuals testified, but the proceedings centered on the Cosgrove-Fletcher confrontation. Unlike a courtroom, the hearing was conducted in an informal setting that allowed speakers

Left: Ed Fletcher dueled with Cosgrove and Kettner over river rights at the 1918 Congressional hearings. *City of San Diego Office of City Clerk, Archives and Records Management.*

Right: San Diego congressman William Kettner sponsored the El Capitan Act and defended the city's position on the river during a 1918 Congressional hearing. *Library of Congress, Prints and Photos Division.*

considerable latitude. The respective presentations were a contrast in style and attitude. The bespectacled, scholarly Cosgrove relied on well-crafted legal arguments he presented in his calm and methodical manner, as well as his pugnacious attitude. The open, affable Fletcher banked on his salesman personality and passion. Both were confident that their position would prevail.

Cosgrove opened for the city with a benign explanation of the city's need to conserve the river water for the public good. But he also wove into his rhetoric the impression that Fletcher and the CWC were focused on private gain rather than civic improvement. Cosgrove reasoned that where any agency regulated a natural resource, the public good took precedent over private interest and intimated that Fletcher and the CWC intended to control the river water for financial gain rather than civic enhancement. Kettner followed and continued the mantra that the city would use the river water for the public interest. The congressman pragmatically detailed San Diego's need for water to support the increasing population and the town's future capacity to thrive. Kettner also expressed the town's quest for water in the broader narrative of national interest. Control of the river offered San Diego the possibility of a stable water supply to support the imminent arrival of the U.S. Navy and the associated federal agencies.

Fletcher prefaced his opening statements with the concession that he was at a distinct disadvantage speaking as a private individual for a private entity against a municipality, but hoped that the members would apply common sense and accept the validity of his arguments. Then the gloves came off. Fletcher attempted to frame the city's actions as both excessive and oppressive. It was a case where a powerful public bureaucracy was attempting to squelch private opportunity. Fletcher took advantage of the informal setting and freely used veiled threats and innuendo to discredit city officials and insinuated that municipal agents knowingly used surreptitious means and political extortion to gain possession of his privately owned dam site property. Fletcher alleged that the city's hidden agenda was a case of civic blackmail designed to seize control of the CWC and secure a dam site without compensation.

Fletcher intimated that the city marginalized the CWC. He boldly averred that his well-managed private enterprise could develop the river quicker and more efficiently than hidebound city bureaucrats and efficiently serve the city's water needs. Fletcher ignored the CWC's financial woes and physical condition and, while offering few details, said that if the CWC developed the upper reaches of the river, the CWC would not displace the tribes on the El Capitan Grande Reservation from their ancestral lands. Fletcher also offered an argument of adverse possession based on years of use by the San Diego Flume and the CWC, as well as the estimated $500,000 the owners had invested to improve the system.

In a glimpse of future legal maneuvering, Fletcher used the moment to denigrate the pueblo rights theory. He pointed out that a San Diego judge had rejected the theory several years previously. Fletcher argued that city decision-makers used a mythical theory, not concrete evidence, ignored facts and allowed petty politics and personal animosity to obstruct common sense in their attempt to prove the city's right to the river. To Fletcher, the facts were clear: the CWC had a legitimate right to the river waters, and the city arrogantly and unjustly impinged on that claim. For Fletcher to assume an attitude other than this would have been uncharacteristic of the man.

The hearing was a major story back in San Diego. Fletcher and Cosgrove kept their respective supporters abreast of the developments with daily accounts. In typical small-town fashion, the coverage of the hearing in local rival newspapers echoed the Fletcher-city rift. Fletcher referred to the city attorney as a camouflage artist who routinely misstated facts to suit his purpose. Cosgrove accused Fletcher of frequently using the press to "jump" on him, both personally and professionally. A self-assured Cosgrove shrugged off the accusations as so far removed from the truth to bother him and retorted that since the city representatives had "walked all over" Fletcher at the hearing, he felt no need to respond to the attacks.[8]

For all the drama, the hearing ended anticlimactically. The committee members heard the arguments and pondered the ramifications but offered no official conclusions. When Cosgrove stated at the close of the meetings that at this time the city had no intention of interfering or altering the CWC's use of the river water and reassured the panel that the city would not take any river water until it passed through the CWC system, Fletcher dropped his opposition. The decision of the city attorney and the Common Council not to pursue the matter tacitly demonstrated that the city officials opted to demur any action until a time, and a courtroom, of their choosing. The hearing was simply a sounding board. Fletcher left the hearing with the sense that the city's reticence to proceed validated the CWC's position and confident that the inevitable litigation would settle the river fight in the CWC's favor. Cosgrove departed with similar confidence. Almost as an aside, and more meaningful than any consequences of the hearing, before departing Washington, Cosgrove sent a telegram to Mayor Louis Wilde and the Common Council noting that the passage of Kettner's El Capitan bill was assured.

THE PARAMOUNT RIGHT TO THE RIVER

In the years following the hearing, city water bureaucrats continued their combative stance on control of the river. In October 1921, a group of city councilmen issued an unofficial statement that declared that "neither outside individuals nor organizations" shall interfere with the rights of the City of San Diego to the waters of the San Diego River. The council also passed a resolution that authorized the city attorney to contest any interference with the city plans to develop the river at El Capitan or Mission Gorge. Councilman Fred Heilbron (referencing the La Mesa, Lemon Grove and Spring Valley Irrigation District) boldly asserted that the river flowed through a city that had long ago claimed a right to the river and that the council was "not going to permit any other community to step in and take it from us."[9] When Fletcher filed a motion with the State Water Commission to appropriate rights to the river waters in January 1922, the city promptly filed suit in San Diego Superior Court to squelch the action and issued a city resolution that declared the city would litigate to protect its right to the river. Later, when the California Department of Public Works issued a certificate of convenience to the CWC granting the right to operate as a public utility, the new city attorney, Shelley Higgins, filed a protest to have an application on record that averred that water cases were settled in the courtroom, not by state commissions.

In May 1924, the City of San Diego and the CWC finally met in the courtroom. In the San Diego Superior Court, Judge C.N. Andrews presided over the case the city brought to condemn two hundred acres of land that the CWC owned at the El Capitan site. This was a bench trial where the judge, not a jury, was the arbiter. To support Higgins and his assistant Arthur F.H. Wright, the city contracted with the law firm that former city attorney Cosgrove now worked for in Los Angeles. Fletcher relied on his personal attorney, Charles Crouch, to lead the CWC defense.

Before the contestants entered the courtroom, Fletcher opened a campaign to try the case in the court of public opinion. Fletcher attempted to use his popularity and personal relationships to keep his side of the case in the public venue. Through daily press releases, Fletcher mocked the case as waste of the city's money and quipped that the city had no more chance of winning the case than he did of becoming president of the United States. Fletcher also added the rejoinder that Cosgrove, currently living and working in Los Angeles, was now a financially motivated outsider with no investment in San Diego's affairs. In his public relations campaign, Fletcher explained that with the evidence his legal team had gathered and his experience in water matters, they would prevail and easily nullify the "ridiculous, ill-founded pueblo theory."[10]

The case proceeded routinely until January 1925, when Judge Andrews unexpectedly allowed the La Mesa, Lemon Grove and Spring Valley Irrigation District to become a litigant in the case. Andrews entertained the request because Fletcher, as the successor in interest to the CWC, was in the process of selling the CWC to the Irrigation District. Likewise, Andrews permitted the City of El Cajon to join the proceedings as an intervener, a party with a relevant interest in the case. In a concession to the City of San Diego, the judge allowed Cosgrove to amend and broaden the city's

Special Consultant Terence Cosgrove (*middle*) and City Attorney Shelly Higgins (*far right*) and his assistant Arthur H. Wright represented the city in the courtroom battle to secure the river for the city. *San Diego History Center.*

complaint against the CWC. Andrews's decisions altered the parameters of the case. The city now contended with the CWC, a private corporation, a municipal irrigation district and another municipality.

Judge Andrews eventually dismissed what locals called the "paramount case" without prejudice, which meant with no decision. The case could now return to another court. Higgins immediately filed a new lawsuit. With Judge Marvin W. Conkling's prior experience on the El Capitan condemnation case, California governor Friend Richardson appointed him to preside over the next proceeding. Aware of the judge's ties to San Diego, the defense immediately attempted to have Conkling recused, but the maneuver failed and the sides agreed to abide by whatever decision Conkling rendered. The litigants reconvened in Orange County in June 1925, with Crouch and Higgins again the lead counsels. Neither party introduced any new information, as they reiterated their respective body of arguments. After years of legal competition, familiarity bred a degree of contempt. Higgins noted that as was Crouch's habit, the lawyer appeared in court with his slight frame dramatically encased in an "overlong swallow-tail coat." During the proceedings, Crouch sarcastically translated El Capitan to mean "the leaders of a band of robbers."[11]

The lawyers argued, and Judge Conkling adjudicated on two issues. The first was the right and necessity of the City of San Diego to condemn two hundred acres at the El Capitan dam site under eminent domain. The second was the question of damages and compensation to the CWC in the event the court allowed condemnation. Conkling's decision carried meaningful ramifications. At this point, two different owners, the city and the CWC, shared parts of the same site, and neither could build a dam without the concurrence of the other. Conkling would decide the first question, and a jury would decide the second.

Conkling delivered his decision on March 2, 1926. He found that the city had not forfeited its right to the river through lack of action and declared the city's case valid. City agents could now gain the El Capitan site by condemnation and, more importantly, possessed the prior and paramount right to the waters of the San Diego River. The

Charles Couch, Fletcher's friend and personal lawyer, led the Cuyamaca Water Company's legal team. *From Ed Fletcher's Memoirs.*

decision granted the city the rights to the river but did not determine the quantity of water the municipality could take. The judge deemed that the CWC, which the La Mesa, Lemon Grove and Spring Valley Irrigation District had purchased from Fletcher in January, was entitled to a portion of the river the city did not need and granted the new owners twenty-seven cubic feet per second of river water. Politically, the city had no desire to antagonize the east county communities and riparian owners dependent on river water so did not challenge the district's right to divert river water. In his closing statement, Conkling urged the parties to meet and negotiate a compromise.

Conkling ordered a separate jury trial to determine the damages from the condemnation due the CWC. Higgins anticipated a $10,000 settlement, but the jury awarded the CWC $600,000. Higgins objected that the amount was excessive. Conkling agreed and recommended a new jury trial to consider a revised settlement.

Conkling's decision offered conciliation rather than resolution. The court acknowledged the city's position as paramount owner of the river but ordered the city to apportion water to the defendants. Neither party was interested in compromise nor satisfied with the court's apparent non-decision. The defense immediately initiated the appeal process. The Second District Court of Appeals heard the appeal, refused the city's motion to dismiss the appeal and referred the case to the California Supreme Court.

The California Supreme Court ended decades of disagreement on March 21, 1930. The seven-member superior court panel determined that the case centered on the right to the river water, not the amount taken. The panel members acknowledged that the La Mesa Irrigation District and the river basin landowners were indeed riparian consumers, but they also accepted the pueblo theory, which made the city the paramount user on the river. The court declared that the San Diego River and all its tributaries belonged to the city. The court also confirmed Conkling's recommendation for a new trial to assign compensation for condemnation damages. In October 1930, the U.S. Supreme Court refused to hear the case, upholding the California Supreme Court's decision that the city controlled the river. The city legal team celebrated, the opposition pondered the implications and most San Diegans expressed relief.

The court decision moved the disagreement between the City of San Diego and the La Mesa, Lemon Grove and Spring Irrigation District out of the courtroom and into the meeting room. As the negotiations between the

Mayor John Bacon, Hiram Savage, Fred Rhodes, Shelley Higgins and several city councilmen in Colterville, California, on a tour of the state's waterworks in 1921. *City of San Diego Office of City Clerk, Archives and Records Management.*

141

city and the district stretched into late 1931, the irrigation district's attorney Albert J. Lee and City Attorney Clinton L. Buyers pressed their respective clients to sign the terms and end the quarreling. Despite the urgency, the negotiations continued at a leisurely bureaucratic pace. Finally, in December 1931, the two parties ended the legal imbroglio. To possess the irrigation district's lands at El Capitan and gain five thousand acre-feet of storage in Murray Reservoir, city negotiators agreed to store irrigation district water in El Capitan Reservoir, granted the district approximately 2 million gallons per day of river water and allowed the irrigation district to convey water through the El Capitan–Lakeside pipeline to its El Monte pumping plant. In a moment of equanimity, the city and district agreed to share the costs of a new delivery pipeline. After years of conflict, the irrigation district lost the decision but won its water.

The city took possession of the entire Mission Gorge in 1931 and the El Capitan site in February 1932 and signed contracts for the construction of El Capitan Dam in April 1932. With the El Capitan Dam project on the horizon, many water experts and most citizens believed that with the city in control of the river, the town's water future was finally secure.

Chapter 10

THE EL CAPITAN DAM

*El Capitan Reservoir as it will appear when full of fresh, pure, unadulterated,
sparkling, clear, and cold mountain water.*
—caption from a 1924 promotional silent movie

The construction of El Capitan Dam, the county's largest dam on its largest river, was almost anti-climactic compared to the struggle to secure the rights to the river and determine the dam site. But with the resolution of those issues, in December 1931 California State Engineer Edward Hyatt approved the project. Hyatt's endorsement put the project in the hands of the city and also preempted the La Mesa, Lemon Grove and Spring Valley Irrigation District from a final legal attempt to dispute San Diego's right to the river.

In their excitement to move the project forward, and even before the city had secured final funding, city officials organized a groundbreaking ceremony on December 24, 1931. Addressing the work crew, a group of city officials and even El Capitan nemesis Ed Fletcher, Mayor Walter Austin spoke of the years of heart-breaking dissension and struggle that had led to this moment and then drove a spade to the riverbed to confirm the project's reality. A more meaningful celebration came a year later, in December 1932, when the Federal Reconstruction Finance Board agreed to purchase $2,350,000 of El Capitan bonds. City officials now authorized Savage, secure in his position with the city and who had set aside his advocacy for a gorge dam, to open construction.

Mayor Walter Austin hosted the El Capitan groundbreaking ceremony in December 1931. *City of San Diego Water Department Archive.*

In April 1932, Savage and the council members opened and reviewed bids from five contractors. The submissions ranged from $3,633,271 from Foley Brothers of St. Paul, Minnesota, to the low of $2,332,860 from Rohl and Connolly of Los Angeles. After a week of deliberation, on the recommendation of Savage and City Attorney C.L. Byer, the council selected Rohl and Connolly as the contractors. Tom Connolly, a tunnel expert, and Wilhelm Rohl, owner of a heavy equipment business, had merged their companies to bid on their first dam construction venture. Given the divisive history of the project, there was little surprise that when the council announced the selection, the owners of a local company bidding on the project immediately disputed the decision and brought a lawsuit. Savage had earlier dismissed the bid of Daley-Fenton because it had not come through formal channels. The Daley-Fenton attorneys argued that the designs the city engineers prepared for bidding were insufficient and that the city should reopen the process. After brief judicial consideration, Judge C.N. Andrews rejected the injunction, and Savage released Rohl and Connolly to open work.

In an unanticipated political move just weeks before the city began construction, the new city manager, A.V. Goeddel, a longtime Savage rival, attempted to maneuver Savage from his position as city hydrologist. Goeddel unilaterally appointed a transparently anti-Savage three-person City Advisory Water Commission to evaluate Savage's position with the city. One of the commissioners, Charles Chandler, was intimately involved in Savage's firing in 1923. Goeddel suggested that the council reassign Savage to only oversee El Capitan, which would effectively remove him from a decision-making role in the city's water planning. The Common Council members rejected the blatantly overt political gambit, and Savage remained the city water chief and in charge of the El Capitan project.

The physicality of the massive dam obliged engineers to select a site appropriate to its scope. State of California surveyors perused the earlier surveys, and undoubtedly mindful that a river flood had caused the Otay Dam failure only fifteen years earlier and the more recent structural collapse of the St. Francis Dam, they chose a location in the granite-lined valley river basin that featured deep bedrock with excellent rock texture. The site sat beneath 3,675-foot-high El Cajon Mountain and just below the confluence of the San Diego River and Conejos Creek, a major tributary. The location offered suitable quarry sites nearby, an open area for the construction camp and sufficient space behind the dam to support an appropriate-sized storage reservoir and allowed workers and equipment easy roadway access. Savage and his staff realized that the dam's position on the middle river offered only limited flood control for the downriver communities but agreed with the state surveyors that the site's other assets outweighed that drawback.

El Capitan would be one of the world's largest dams. Most hydraulic engineers in the early twentieth century believed that large gravity dams, which depended on the structure's weight for stability, were the safest structures. The project engineers designed El Capitan as a semi-hydraulic rock embankment structure with an impervious clay core. The 1,500-foot span between the canyon walls and the composition of foundation rock influenced the decision to construct a fill dam. A contextual technological factor was the construction equipment available. The contractors did not have access to large tractors and trucks when the engineers settled on the design in the late 1920s, which explained the choice of the hydraulic fill method where laborers could move large qualities of material as a water-based medium.

The construction of dams using the hydraulic-fill method started in the 1890s, and by the 1920s, most engineers, though not all, considered the method safe and reliable. Mr. D.W. Albert supervised the hydraulic application at El Capitan. In the hydraulic method, workers created upstream

Above: Engineers constructed El Capitan, one of the world's largest embankment dams, using the hydraulic fill method. *City of San Diego Water Department Archive.*

Opposite: The transmission pipeline, completed in two phases in 1926 and 1935, conveyed water from the reservoir to the city distributing plant. *City of San Diego Water Department Archive.*

and downstream concrete embankments, called toe walls, that extended to the bedrock foundation and then filled the middle area, the puddle core, with saturated hydraulic material. Water sprayed under pressure on earthen slopes melted the surface material away and created a solution of wet viscous substance that settled into an impervious clay medium in the interior core. The engineers encapsulated the top of the dam with rock and gravel to seal the core. To prevent any water from percolating under the dam, engineers placed a steel-reinforced concrete cutoff wall in the middle of the puddle core and sealed the wall with concrete grout. Engineers diverted the river through the construction site via a twenty-five-foot concrete-lined, horseshoe-shaped bypass tunnel near the south abutment. When the dam was completed, workers sealed the bypass tunnel with a solid concrete plug, and the reservoir was ready to receive and store water.

The dam's rock-studded downstream face and broad crest were the symbols of the project, but the distribution system was its heart. The 1924 election included bonds to construct a steel thirty-six-inch pipeline to transport water twenty-five miles from the Lakeside pump house to the University Heights

filtration plant, which the city completed in 1927–28. At the same time, city engineers designed a two-mile-long pipeline that connected the El Monte Pumping Plant to the plant in Lakeside. A six-mile-long line conveyed water from El Capitan to the La Mesa, Lemon Grove and Spring Valley Irrigation District's pumping facility in El Monte. This was a state-of-the-art water supply system.

Constructing the Dam

El Capitan's remote location, some eight miles east of the town of Lakeside and almost thirty miles from downtown San Diego, required a sizable construction camp to house workers and staff. There were actually two camps. The camp on the south side of the river, about one half mile downstream from the dam site on U.S. Forest Service land, housed the city forces, the resident engineer and his assistants, survey crews and bookkeepers. To save money, Savage ordered a city crew to disassemble and transport some of the buildings from the abandoned Sutherland Dam site. The contractor's camp

The contractors housed the workers in on-site facilities that offered room and board. *City of San Diego Water Department Archive.*

sat on the north side of the river. The wood-frame buildings offered the amenities for semi-permanent living that included a bunkhouse, bathhouse, mess hall, warehouse, shops and offices for the city and contractor staff. At the end of the project, in December 1934, a private construction company paid the city $900 for the camps as they stood. The San Diego Police Department took possession of the contractor's camp, which later served as an Italian prisoner of war center in World War II and then became a Police Department Alcohol Rehabilitation Center. Eventually, the city dismantled all the buildings except for two small structures of the city camp that became the homes for the subsequent reservoir-keepers into the mid-1990s.

Contractors Rohl and Connolly required all workers to live in the construction camp. Obligating the men to stay in the company camp was an efficient way to monitor the workers and prevent another private enterprise from building a competing resident encampment. From their $5.00 daily wage, each worker paid $1.75 for board, lodging, blankets and pillows, an amount that essentially covered the company's expenses. Concerned over the legality of the housing practice, the Common Council asked City Attorney Byers his opinion on the arrangement. Byers apparently condoned the agreement, for the practice continued throughout the course of the project. As happened at the isolated Morena and Barrett Dam projects in

The contractors brought in performers and singers to entertain workers in the remote construction site. *City of San Diego Water Department Archive.*

the 1920s, wives and families unofficially filtered out to El Capitan. To boost morale, the contractors and the city regularly brought in singing groups and theatrical troupes to entertain the isolated workers.

El Capitan was a Depression-era project that offered the city a unique opportunity. In January 1932, a year before the project opened, the council had passed a city ordinance that decried the serious menace of unemployment and passed a $5,000 appropriation to create jobs. With federal funding in hand, community leaders saw the dam project as a vehicle to boost regional employment. The information package to the bidding contractors emphasized that in addition to bringing water to the city, the project was also intended to relieve unemployment. Goeddel and the council embraced the citizen-laborer concept. To ensure that locals had a priority for the jobs, the council required the contractor to hire only individuals who had resided in San Diego for at least one year. The council assigned Rudolph C. Wueste, the supervisor of the city reservoir system, to review all applications to ensure that the job seekers met the citizenship qualifications. Wueste scrutinized the paperwork and then met with the contractors' legal representative to determine if prospective employees met city charter and City Public Works standards. At a time when the minimum wage was generally twenty-five cents an hour, at the recommendation of Savage and Goeddel, a Common Council resolution set the minimum wage for El Capitan workers at $5 per day.

Despite the apparent favorable employment conditions, in July 1932 questions arose regarding job site labor and housing conditions, and the Common Council opened an inquiry. The public meeting—which included the seven-person Common Council, City Manager Goeddel and various speakers—occurred before a "vociferous gallery" that booed and cheered as the speakers presented their respective views. The labor issue centered on the number of nonresident laborers the contractors had allegedly hired. The resident numbers John M. Martin, the representative for the contractors, provided the council did not match those of City Inspector Joseph H. Hamil. Hamil indicated that his data suggested that a large proportion of the men on the job were not San Diego residents, as the contract required. Martin denied that claim but offered no evidence to support his position. Martin also denied the allegation that the contractors profited from the room and board charges they levied on the workers. Martin was met with a "chorus of boos" when he explained that there were certain jobs that required workers with specialized skills that San Diego workers did not possess. When Martin hesitated to speak to the other issues, Councilman Bennett threatened to abrogate the contract. After hours of debate, the proceedings reached an impasse when a flustered Martin suddenly announced that he was not authorized to comment on the issues the council wished to investigate.[1] The council ended the evening with a call for a follow-up meeting and vowed to thoroughly investigate the situation. The labor debates continued into September, when an exasperated Goeddel told the contractors that he would withhold payments for work and materials until the parties settled the labor disputes. Within days, the city and the contractors announced that they had settled the differences and work resumed.

The dam project was the talk of the town. As was common in this era, the city encouraged and welcomed visitors to the construction site. Savage submitted weekly reports to the mayor, the council and the chamber of commerce that detailed the visits of outside groups. The guests included local dignitaries, delegations from the navy, women's civic organizations, staff from the local State College and members of local business clubs.

The city and contractors allowed hundreds of people to visit the job site during construction. *City of San Diego Water Department Archive.*

The visitors arrived in groups from ten to one hundred. Savage welcomed one and all, frequently led guided tours and often posed for photographs. Politicians used the occasions, which usually involved a staged photograph with Savage, as an opportunity to show their constituents that they were part of an important public enterprise. Professionals, particularly other civil engineers, trekked out to the site to kibitz with their peers, scrutinize the work and observe the construction techniques. Prominent visitors often stayed overnight in the city camp guesthouse. All came to watch the massive dam rise out of the remote river valley.

The city undertook the construction of El Capitan Dam when hardy men with shovels and picks labored alongside the steam-operated equipment and bulldozers and trucks. State agencies had vastly improved safety protocols since the early days of dam construction, but workers still toiled in an accident-rich environment. The California State Industrial Accident Commission, an agency established to administer the Workers Compensation Act, prescribed safety regulations, required the contractors to furnish the city with a certificate of insurance covering all employees and monitored the project with regular on-site safety inspections. The commission's reports noted that the most recurring infraction at El Capitan

Community leaders hoped that the construction of El Capitan Dam would end civic division and solve the town's water problems. *City of San Diego Water Department Archive.*

involved the integrity of the magazine where workers stored dynamite, which inspectors consistently insisted was not fireproof.

The fact that there were not more serious injuries was a testament to the constitution of the workingmen or a mark of luck. It was physical, often dangerous work. The uniform of the day for most workers was leather shoes, work pants, a cotton shirt, warm jackets in the winter and a soft hat to fend off the sun, serve as a sweat band or keep your head warm. The state required construction engineers to issue Ten-Day Reports, a general account of the work for that period, which called out any on-the-job injuries. The reports from El Capitan typically included scratches, bruises and the occasional serious injury, most often a broken bone. Two deaths occurred at the site in the quarry, one when a worker fell from a utility pole and one resulting from a tunnel-blasting incident.[2] Dangerous or not, most local men were pleased to have the opportunity to work and earn a wage.

In addition to individual employment possibilities, city leaders also hoped that the project would serve as a local economic windfall. The council lobbied the project contractors to solicit San Diego banks to handle monetary transactions and San Diego merchants to be their first choice for materials, supplies, machinery and tools. When Savage received authorization to clear away brush and dead and fallen trees from the dam and reservoir sites, the

Workers in this Depression-era project labored under difficult and dangerous conditions.
City of San Diego Water Department Archive.

council permitted the public to come in and carry away any fallen trees for their own use or resale. The city hired fifty men and allowed citizens to cut standing timber with the caveat that they deliver one in five loads to the Salvation Army, a requirement that interestingly met with grudging acceptance and proved difficult to enforce. When Savage and the general contractors asked to improve the road between El Monte and the job site, the council ordered the contractor to hire only local men.

The city's strategy to hire local unemployed citizens proved a success. In September 1932, City Manager Goeddel informed Mayor John Forward and the council that 80 percent of the nearly 330 workers lived locally. When the councilmen questioned Savage about the disposition of the other 20 percent, he replied that certain positions—such as truck drivers, electricians, blasters and welders—required individuals with specialized skills, expertise often not found among San Diego citizens. In the latter stages of the project, City Labor Inspector Thomas L. Knott sent Savage a memo that indicated of the 175 workers on the job, 133 were county residents, 27 were former residents who currently lived near the site and 15 were skilled "key men."[3] The council, concerned that the city hire as many of the local unemployed as possible, acted on Savage's recommendation, and every ten days the contractor rotated a new set of unemployed men into the unskilled positions. The eclectic labor force at the dam site eventually included former soldiers and sailors and prisoners from local jails. Over the course of the project, the rotation system employed an estimated 4,000 individuals out of San Diego's population of approximately 210,000, which relieved unemployment and boosted the regional economy.

The El Capitan project created a competitive job market but also fostered evidence of discrimination. In the context of extant racial prejudice, the city and the contractors employed white laborers before others. But the slight did not go uncontested. In September 1932, San Diego councilman Dan Rossi complained to Mayor John Forward about the "apparent discrimination" against employing Black workers. Rossi argued that these men were citizens, taxpayers and homeowners who suffered the same economic hardships as others in town and asked the mayor to correct the unfair situation. Forward queried Savage, who responded that while the city could not legally require the contractors to hire African Americans, he had repeatedly and respectfully suggested they do so. While it was unsubstantiated, an item in the magazine *Opportunity* complained that the El Capitan project employed hundreds of men in various capacities but hired no African American workers.[4] The San Diego African American community was not satisfied with the hiring policy.

In an early September 1932 council meeting, several groups confronted the council and City Manager Goeddel regarding hiring practices at El Capitan. At the meeting, representatives from the Logan Heights Unemployment Council proposed that one of every ten men that the contractors employed "be of the negro race." They also demanded that contractors not segregate the Black workers from the other laborers at the job site. The speakers expressed dissatisfaction with the council's explanation that the contract only stipulated that Rohl and Connolly hire San Diego laborers and that the council had no "control over the kind of citizens" the contractors hired. Following an inquiry, Goeddel announced that he believed Rohl and Connolly indeed had discriminated against African American workers, but in his report to the council on September 17, he conceded that according to the contact with Rohl and Connolly, the council could not force the contractors to hire "colored labor."[5]

Suffering from the general malaise of the Great Depression, local Native Americans also faced their employment dilemmas. Still not settled on new lands, the leaders of the El Capitan Grande Indians requested jobs at the dam site. In late 1931, speaking for the reservation's Indian Committee, Ramon Ames and twenty band members petitioned the city for employment to overcome the hardship resettlement brought on the tribe. Ames asserted that the project caused the band's unstable circumstances, which entitled the Indians to employment. The council asked Savage to investigate the situation. The engineer responded that he had twice met with the regional superintendent of Indian reservations and recommended that the city hire Indians. Congress granted all native-born American Indians citizenship in 1924, but as Savage noted, the contractors maintained that for them to employ Indians, the council would need to modify the city resolution that mandated the contractors hire only San Diegans. In October 1932, the city's resident engineer, Harold Wood, suggested to Savage that the city make arrangements for the Indians to perform clearing work due to start in November.[6] It is possible that some American Indians worked on the project that displaced them, but whether any of the band members actually gained employment on the project remains uncertain.

EL CAPITAN DAM

The massive El Capitan Dam created the city's largest storage reservoir. When completed in December 1934 (about the same time San Francisco started receiving water from its Hetch Hetchy project), the 237-foot-tall structure, mere feet from being the tallest dam in the world, created a 1,580-surface-acre reservoir storing approximately 112,800 acre-feet or 39 billion gallons of water. But as the dam project progressed, the completion of the conveyance system actually spawned a minor dilemma.

In early 1926, the city had completed construction of the seventeen-mile section of pipeline that ran from Lakeside to the city plant at University Heights. The construction of this segment of pipeline, under the provisions of the 1924 bond initiative, clearly indicated the commitment and expectation of city leaders that the El Capitan project would be completed. But then the project appeared in jeopardy when city voters rejected a bond that funded the pipeline section that connected El Capitan Reservoir to Lakeside. Frantic to complete the transmission line, Mayor Percy J. Benbough authorized City Hydraulic Engineer Fred Rhodes to contact the federal Public Works Administration for assistance. Through Rhodes, the city offered to pay 70 percent of the $430,000 construction costs if the Public Works Administration would fund the remainder, approximately $129,000. After negotiations and legal assurances from the city, in March 1936 Mayor Benbough signed the agreement, and the project went forward. With the forty-eight-inch steel pipeline completed, the El Capitan Reservoir had the capacity to supply the city 10 million gallons of water per day.

The engineers expected that when filled, the reservoir would extend eight miles upstream into the river valley. In the winter of 1935, fifteen inches of rain fell in the San Diego River watershed, but the drought-parched ground absorbed most of the downpour and left the reservoir only partially filled.

El Capitan Reservoir filled for the first time in 1938 and overflowed down the spillway by the San Diego Police Rehabilitation Camp. *San Diego Police Historical Society.*

Not until March 1938 would the reservoir fill to capacity. To most citizens, that moment validated the project, but many water professionals recognized the moment as a temporary achievement.

At the end of November 1934, Rohl and Connolly and local contractor M.H. Golden completed their respective assignments, and on December 1, the Bodenhamer Construction Company finished the final piece of work, a spillway extension. Three days later, on December 4, the City Council officially accepted the dam for the city. Within the project's $5,790,070 budget, the dam itself accounted for $2,705,003.

The city officially invited the people of San Diego to join in the dedication of the dam on February 22, 1935. The day before the ceremony, city workers graded parking spaces at the base of the dam and on the upper spillway, installed a mechanical amplification sound system, erected a wooden speakers platform on the north end of the dam's crest and cordoned off restricted areas. That Friday dawned warm and clear for the 10:00 a.m. ceremony. Some 1,200 people took the thirty-mile trek along the dusty back roads for the celebration, and another 1,000 drifted out to see the dam during the day. The guests climbed to the dam's wide crest, some just wandered about, some took guided tours and then they all gathered before the stage erected near the spillway to hear the presentations. The crowd was so large that many listened to the presentation while standing in the lower parking area.

City organizers realized that the ceremony provided the perfect setting to dispel decades of public discord, heal old wounds and foster reconciliation. The speakers' messages articulated the political convolution of the dam's history but also the need to reconnect as a community. The program chairman, Albert V. Mayhofer, chairman of the City Water Commission, introduced Mayor Albert W. Bennett, who gave a brief statement and then welcomed Monsignor John M. Hegarty, whom Mayhofer called a man from the same faith of the padres who first developed the river. In his talk, Hegarty pleaded with San Diego citizens to "mellow the partisanship" that had divided the community for so long. Fred Pyle, Savage's assistant and the project manager in the dam's final stages, presented a message that stressed the importance of the dam and Savage's vital role in the project, ironically one that Savage had argued against for years. Speakers included several oppositional figures, specifically Chester Harriett, the general manager of the La Mesa Irrigation District, and Ed Fletcher. Although he was not listed in the official program, Fletcher, who battled against the dam for twenty years and was now a state senator, spoke about past

Hundreds of people parked their cars at the base of the dam on dedication day. *City of San Diego Water Department Archive.*

mistakes in local water development and pledged support of future water enterprises. Mayhofer then called on the keynote speaker, former city attorney Terence Cosgrove, Special Water Counsel to the city. Cosgrove commented that "for years the project was close to failure," but he noted that once agreed on it received the wholehearted support of the people. Cosgrove also recalled the service of Hiram Savage, who had died in June 1934 just months before the completion of the dam. In his last days in the hospital, Savage met with project managers, consulted engineering reports and avidly followed the dam's progress. (The city later renamed Otay Dam Savage Dam in his honor.) Cosgrove concluded that of all the dams in San Diego County, none had met with "such sincere and honest opposition as did this structure." Cosgrove said with the project now completed, it was time for the citizens to reunite.[7]

Following the speeches, Cosgrove unveiled the brass dedication plaque. Ironically, the plaque bore the names of an acting mayor, a new city manager and several individuals who actively opposed the project, but no names of the project's early advocates. After revealing the plaque, Cosgrove invited the assembled onlookers to wander the site to contemplate the colossal nature of the structure and reflect on the fact that after decades of contention, the people of San Diego finally had their river dam and reservoir.

Unforeseen Consequences

In the city's scramble to enhance its water supply, the presence of the El Capitan Dam created several unanticipated effects. As intended, the dam provided incidental flood control and made the development of downstream roads, commercial businesses and residence possible, but it also altered the riparian ecosystem, based on the river's patterns of recharging its groundwater beds. Less river runoff meant the absorption of less water into the subterranean basins. The reduction of groundwater supplies adversely affected the water level in the wells of ranchers, farmers and domestic users in El Monte Valley; the amount of water the La Mesa, Lemon Grove and Spring Valley Water District pumped from the Flume system; and also the volume of water available to the City of San Diego's pumping properties near the Lakeside area and the El Monte Valley. In a historic aside, irrigation district engineers also removed the portion of the Flume running between the dam and the El Monte pumping station from operation, thus ending the San Diego Flume's more than four decades of continuous service from the upper river.

Citizens gathered on the crest of the huge dam for the official dedication ceremony in February 1935. *City of San Diego Water Department Archive.*

RECORD OF
H.N. SAVAGE
BARRETT DAM
OTAY DAM
SWEETWATER DAM
EL CAPITAN DAM

Hiram Savage supervised the El Capitan project until his death in 1934. *From the* San Diego Union, *June 1934.*

After the dedication ceremony, guests were allowed to wander over the massive dam. *City of San Diego Water Department Archive.*

The massive dam dramatically permanently altered the river's hydrology. Before El Capitan, even with the small Flume diverting dam on the upper river, the San Diego River was essentially a free-flowing water course. That changed when El Capitan Dam impounded the river. The El Capitan Reservoir covered 1,580-surface acres, which consumed the original river channel and reconfigured the riverbed for miles above the dam. The diversions into El Capitan Reservoir affected the annual cycles of high runoff and low base flows and the movement of sediment in the river, shifted the river's channel, modified the vegetation along the river and affected the recharge of downstream groundwater.

The dam also reshaped the lives of the people the reservoir waters displaced. When the city first proposed a dam at El Capitan, the Department of the Interior initially demurred any decision on transferring federal property to a municipality (an issue the San Diego Flume Company ignored in 1886) but eventually accepted the importance of the project to the growth of the town. With the sanction of the federal government, the city superseded the rights of the tribes on the Capitan Grande Indian Reservation. In 1919, Congress passed the El Capitan Act, which allocated $361,420 to permit the City of San Diego to acquire 1,904 acres on the El Capitan Grande

Indian Reservation and relocate the tribes affected. The city purchased an additional 920 acres of reservation land for $35,507 in 1931.

The city secured land for the dam and reservoir, while the American Indians on the reservation had a predicament. The public dilemma of dispossessing the Indians from the reservation lands appeared as early as 1915. The opposing lawyers in a hearing in Los Angeles that year agreed that removing the El Capitan Indians from the affected land to lands the city selected was a satisfactory solution, but opposition from tribes on the reservation compelled the city to seek Congressional action to secure the desired water rights and lands. The city prevailed through the El Capitan Act of 1919 in which Indian Affairs agents and the Department of the Interior officials approved the relocation of some Capitan Grande bands. By agreement, the Indians had ninety days to vacate their ancestral land once the reservoir started to fill. The displaced bands, about 150 individuals, moved in groups and as individuals to several nearby properties, some to Barona and others eventually to the Viejas Valley. City planners viewed the fate of the inhabitants of the El Capitan Grande Indian Reservation as a collateral byproduct in the city's crusade to secure water. In this case, a municipal aspiration conflicted with an ethical obligation, and the city accepted the displacement as a minor social cost for the greater public good. Despite objections, the tribes had little recourse and were forced to comply. It was an uneven exchange, a case of municipal hubris. The American Indians lost a homeland and a river, and the city had a dam.

The persistent thought that impounding the San Diego River would solve the town's water dilemma was finally tested. In 1934, most San Diegans believed that coupling El Capitan Reservoir with the existing facilities at Morena, Lower Otay and Barrett, and accessing water from Hodges Reservoir, signaled a new era of water security. The day following the dam's dedication ceremony, the *San Diego Union* declared that the dam's completion marked a new era for San Diego. However, reality defied public perception.

As Hiram Savage and Fred Heilbron presciently foresaw, the El Capitan project was a positive accretion in the city's ongoing quest for water sustainability, but not the final step. El Capitan Reservoir became operational at a time when municipal expansion remained tied to the pattern that more water meant more growth. That paradigm changed within five years as San Diego's naturally expanding population outstripped the capacity of the city water system to supply its citizens through county resources. Rather than seeking water to stimulate growth, the city required water to sustain its enlarged population. By the mid-1930s, the town's water gathering strategy had transitioned from a single method, regional impounded reservoirs, to one based on diversity. The river became an ancillary aspect in the town's water infrastructure. The inability of the El Capitan project to fulfill the expectations of water experts coupled with the inadequacy of local resources shifted the county's water model from a hydrologic philosophy that emphasized regional water resources to one centered on water imported from outside sources. The constrained benefits of the El Capitan project tempered the initial sense of technical accomplishment, and rather than a final solution, the dam's limited utility signaled the beginning of the end of the San Diego River's role as a major regional water provider. El Capitan Dam was a symbol of engineering triumph and a means to an end rather than a final resolution.

In 2017, California state inspectors categorized the 83-year-old dam's safety level as fair. The inspectors noted that El Capitan no longer met State of California structural standards and exhibited an extremely high risk for a catastrophic loss of life and property in the event of failure. In January 2018, an independent panel of California dam safety experts placed the onus of dam safety on individual managers and mandated that the City of San Diego maintain the El Capitan Reservoir level at no more than 50 percent capacity. In 2021, California State Division of Dam Safety engineers pronounced three area dams satisfactory and none unsatisfactory, with El Capitan listed in poor condition. In May 2021, San Diego city officials announced a $10 million plan to evaluate the city's nine dams, which ranged in age from 61 to 109 years, which supplied 10 percent of the town's water supply. Into 2022, the City of San Diego continues to explore the restoration of El Capitan Dam. The dam's hydraulic fill construction is at risk of failure in a major earthquake, and the spillway, which has its outfall at the base of the dam allowing floodwaters entering the channel to potentially erode the dam's foundation, requires an overhaul. Given the costs and the city's insouciance, time and nature may well determine the dam's fate.

Epilogue

THE LEGACY RIVER

> *Our mission is to preserve and enhance the San Diego River, its watershed,*
> *and its natural, cultural, and recreational resources.*
> —*San Diego River Park Foundation, 2018*

Water historians measure rivers in terms of natural and human intervention. Such was the case with San Diego and its river. In the town's first eighty American years, the San Diego River was at the heart of the community. San Diegans survived on the river's surface water and groundwater, stemmed the river to protect the harbor, saw the first private entrepreneurial efforts to commercialize the river and experienced years of civic division and legal complications. Through it all, the river evolved and the town grew.

The San Diego River has avoided the fate of disinterest and not suffered the indignity of its sister in Los Angeles. The Corps of Engineers transformed that river from a meandering stream bordered with willows and cottonwoods into a concrete storm drain. Through municipal and community activism, the San Diego River has managed to remain an active, vital watercourse. In the late twentieth and early twenty-first centuries, the management of the river has centered on restoration as a coalition of city and private organizations, namely the San Diego River Park Foundation and the San Diego River Conservancy—an independent, non-regulatory state agency—became the stewards of the river. The organizations have dealt with the issue of the river's water quality, applied governmental

The river offered citizens drinking water and sometimes a place for them to cool off in the heat of the summer. *Ocean Beach Historical Society.*

regulatory controls to protect and restore the river, enhanced the public's awareness of this incredible natural resource and sustained the river as a green belt from its source to its terminus.

In 2022, the river faced old issues and new dilemmas. Cyclical flooding remains a major inconvenience, which, true to San Diego's semi-arid roots, generally occurs following several years of drought. Contemporary flooding cuts the roads connecting the Fashion Valley Mall from the merchants in Mission Valley and occasionally interrupts trolley service passing through the valley. The newest dilemma is how to deal with the litter from the influx of homeless encampments on the tree- and shrub-covered interior islets and the pollution from leaky sewers along the riverbanks in the valley. In December 2017 and again in July 2018, the City of San Diego launched an unprecedented cleanup campaign to protect the river that is a "jewel for all San Diegans."[1] Keeping the river as a community asset has become a holistic community effort.

The San Diego River was never a navigable water course, hence twenty-first-century San Diego is a beach and harbor town, not a river town. Except in times of flood, San Diegans seem to take the river for granted, recognize its existence and publicly appreciate its environmental, economic, recreational and aesthetic amenities. The San Diego River remains a symbol of the city's past and a reflection of the public commitment to the conservation of a valued historical and natural resource.

NOTES

Introduction

1. Smythe, *History of San Diego*, 694.
2. Martin, "Growth by the Gallon."
3. Wright, "History of the San Diego River," Vol. I, 2–5.
4. See Smythe, *Conquest of Arid America*.

Chapter 1

1. "The Rivers of San Diego County, No. III, The San Diego River," *San Diego Union*, January 17, 1875, 3.
2. Shipek, *Pushed into the Rocks*, 18, 24–25.
3. Smythe, *History of San Diego*, 694.
4. Hall, *Irrigation in Southern California*, 1:43.
5. Letter, Serra to Palou, July 3, 1769, in Smythe, *History of San Diego*, 43–45.
6. Letter, Crespi to Father Guardian of San Fernando College in Mexico City, June 22, 1769, in Englehart, *San Diego Mission*, 15–16.
7. See letter, Father Juan Crespi to Father Francisco Palou, June 9, 1769, in Hopkins, *History of San Diego*, 40.
8. Palou, *Historical Memoirs of New California*, 1:100.
9. Ibid., 1:306.

10. U.S. Congress, *Memoir of the San Diego River*; U.S. Congress, *Report to Col. J.J. Abert*, 110–11.
11. Hall, *Irrigation in Southern California*, 1:42–43.

Chapter 2

1. Patterson, "Hatfield the Rain Maker," 3–32.
2. "Angel City Press Corrects False Flood Reports," *San Diego Union*, February 8, 1916, 14; "Flood Damage Yarns Printed in Los Angeles Amply Controverted by Facts as to City's Condition," *San Diego Union*, February 2, 1916, 1; "Letter Writing Day to Shatter False Flood Reports," *San Diego Union*, February 9, 1916, 1.
3. Higgins, *This Fantastic City San Diego*, 181–83.

Chapter 3

1. U.S. Congress, *Report of the United States and Mexico Boundary Survey*, 4; U.S. Congress, Senate, *Coast Survey Showing the Progress of the Survey*, 300.
2. Innis, *San Diego's Legends*, 27–28; Smith, *Story of San Diego*, 7.
3. U.S. Congress. *Memoir of the San Diego River*, 111; "San Diego to Los Angeles," *Los Angeles Times*, March 10, 1882, 3; *San Diego Herald*, September 24, 1853; "Improvement of the San Diego River," *Los Angeles Times*, September 17, 1853, 2; *Phoenixiana*, 200–205; Smith, *Story of San Diego*, 117–23.
4. "An Incident," *San Diego Herald*, October 1, 1853, 3; also see *San Diego Herald*, September 24, 1853, 2.
5. "Turning San Diego River," *San Diego Herald*, December 19, 1868, 2.
6. San Diego Chamber of Commerce, "Annual Report of 1872"; meeting, December 7, 1871, in Journal, April 3, 1871, to March 1887; meeting, November 25, 1874, Journal, April 3, 1871, to March 1887, 35, in the San Diego Chamber of Commerce Regular Meeting Minutes (hereafter cited as SDCCRMM).
7. Secretary of War, *Annual Reports of the Chief of Engineers*, "Mendell Plan," vol. 2, Appendix EE 1, 1875, 631.
8. "The Chinese Question," *San Diego Union*, June 4, 1876, 3.
9. Secretary of War, *Annual Reports of the Chief of Engineers*, 1877, part 2, 998–99.
10. "The Outrage," *San Diego Union*, February 1, 1882, 3.

Chapter 4

1. See Wray, *Notes of the San Diego Flume*; Hall, *Irrigation in Southern California*, 2:68–83.
2. "The San Diego Flume Company," *San Diego Union*, July 13, 1886, 3; "The Largest Flume in the World," *Pacific Rural Press*, November 24, 1888, 441.
3. See Goudey, "Investigation of the Water Supply at San Diego."
4. Helix Water District, "Fast Flume Facts."
5. Hennessey, "Politics of Water in San Diego," 368.
6. Farley, "Cuyamaca Water Company Partnership," 181–202. Also see Strathman, "Land, Water, and Real Estate," 124–44.
7. Letter, Fletcher to R.W. Hawley, February 11, 1914, Fletcher Collection, MS 135, Series XVII, Box 10, Folder 14; "Engineer Report on the Condition the Cuyamaca Flume," March 30, 1925, State of California Railroad Commission, 6.
8. Fletcher, *Memoirs*, 165, 166 and 177; letter, Fletcher to Frank Lane, Secretary of Interior, March 23, 1916, Fletcher Papers, Box 16, Folder 5; letter, Fletcher to Lane, Secretary of Interior, May 10, 1917, Fletcher Papers, Box 16, Folder 5; letter, Fletcher to Huber, January 13, 1922, Fletcher Collection, Box 9, Folder 8, MS 135.
9. Letter, Fletcher to Councilman Heilbron, April 28, 1919, Fletcher Papers, Box 11, Folder 5.
10. "San Diego's Water Rights," *San Diego Union*, March 19, 1918, 4.
11. Wright, "History of the San Diego River," 1:46, 48.

Chapter 5

1. Hall, *Irrigation in Southern California*, 2:83–85.
2. Ibid.
3. "More Water," *San Diego Union*, October 8, 1887, 2.
4. Junipero Land and Water Company Records, MS 237, 27, San Diego History Center.
5. William S. Post, "Report on Boulder Creek Reservoir Site No. 5," February 17, 1913, Fletcher Papers, Box 450, Folder 14.
6. "Councilmen Laugh at Talk by Fletcher of Compromise," *San Diego Union*, March 12, 1918, 8.

7. Letter, E.B. Taylor, Hollywood Movie Supply Company, to Fletcher, July 10, 1929, Fletcher Papers, Box 113, Folder 9.

Chapter 6

1. Letter, Viceroy Bucareli to Father Serra, December 17, 1773, in Green, *San Diego Old Mission Dam*, 7–8.
2. Green, *San Diego Old Mission Dam*, 29–30, 40.
3. Ibid., 29–30.
4. Wray, *Notes of the San Diego Flume*, from the 1920s Water Rights Hearings, "Plan and Purpose of the San Diego Flume," pages 391 and 402 in the document.
5. Hall, *Irrigation in Southern California*, 2:71–72.
6. "Report on Diverting Dam," Post to Fletcher, October 24, 1911, Fletcher Papers, Box 21, Folder 26.

Chapter 7

1. Alastair Bland, "Water Is Life," *CalMatters*, February 27, 2020; "Everything You Need to Know About California's Historic Water Law," *Guardian*, February 27, 2020.
2. See "Water Development in Mission Valley," *San Diego Union*, July 22, 1904; "Deep Wells in Mission Valley," *San Diego Union*, September 4, 1904; "Proposals for Deep Wells," *San Diego Union*, September 29, 1904; "Improving the Water System," *San Diego Union*, March 31, 1904.
3. "Examining Water Lands in El Cajon," *San Diego Union*, October 8, 1904, 3.
4. "Report of C.S. Alverson on the El Cajon Valley Water Investigation," to the Special Water Committee of the Common Council of the City of San Diego, November 28, 1904, 1–3, Fletcher Papers, Box 35, Folder 26.
5. "Cajon Water Supply Is Abundant," *San Diego Union*, December 20, 1904, 6; "Lippincott Says Plan Is Feasible," *San Diego Union*, January 6, 1905, Sec. II, 1, 8.
6. "Disreputable Campaigning," *San Diego Union*, February 19, 1905, 4.
7. "Report of the J. Johnson, Jr. Water System on the San Diego River," C.S. Alverson, Hydraulic Engineer, September 20, 1916, 1–3, 12, Fletcher Papers, Box 35, Folder 32.

8. "Wooden Flume Built to Protect Ranchers," *San Diego Union*, November 25, 1916, 8.

9. Green, "Safe Yield Study," 47; "City of San Diego Operating Department Water Impounding Bureau," Table no. 14, July 20, 1926, R.H. Wueste, Supervisor, in "Safe Yield Study," 71.

10. "Tabulation of Available Data as to the Water Supplied to City of San Diego," January 23, 1915, Fletcher Papers, Box 56, Folder 16.

11. Hundley, *Great Thirst*, 530.

Chapter 8

1. Perry, *History of the Development*, 2–3.

2. Hopkins, *History of San Diego*, 282–83.

3. Land Sales Agreement, William B. Kuhner and Helen D. Kuhner with George Sawday, July 29, 1913, Declaration of Trust, Southern Title Guaranty Company with James Murray and Ed Fletcher, August 13, 1913, Fletcher Papers, Box 61, Folder 1.

4. "Water Company Activities Told by Witness," *San Diego Union*, January 7, 1916, 3; "Resume El Capitan Water Hearings," *Los Angeles Herald*, January 3, 1916, 13.

5. Letter, Fletcher to Lane, 1916, Fletcher Papers, Box 62, Folder 5; letter, Fletcher to Lane, March 23, 1916, and May 19, 1917, Fletcher Papers, Box 16, Folder 5.

6. U.S. Congress, House, *Conservation and Storage of Water*, hearing, 44.

7. San Diego City Ordinance no. 7833, August 25, 1919; San Diego City Council Resolution no. 26403, April 20, 1921.

8. "Build El Capitan Dam, Let Conduit Wait, Says Council," *San Diego Union*, September 23, 1920, 1, 5.

9. "Report to Mayor and Common Council, Relative to the Purchase of the Cuyamaca Water Company and the Construction a Mission Gorge Dam, April 13, 1921," Water Commission of San Diego—Julius Wangenheim, Charles T. Chandler and F.M. White, City of San Diego Water Department Archive.

10. Freeman, "Freeman Report," Document #160932; Pyle, *Feature History*, 5:3,070; Jackson, *Building the Ultimate Dam*, 233.

11. Meeting, September 28, 1924, SDCCRMM, Journal, November 1923–November 1924.

12. "Moody Rips Opposition to Capitan," *San Diego Union*, November 11, 1924, 1, 3; "Advantages of El Capitan Dam," *San Diego Union*, November 13, 1924, 7.

13. "New Angle of Mayor Answered," *San Diego Union*, November 18, 1924; "Hot Water Fight Ends as Voters Visit Polls," *San Diego Sun*, November 18, 1924.

14. "Camera Records Election Pleas," *San Diego Union*, July 11, 1929.

15. "Thomas King Recommendations to the Chamber of Commerce," January 5, 1931, SDCCRMM, Journal, 1931.

16. "Report by Ed Fletcher to the Chamber of Commerce," February 7, 1931, SDCCRMM, Journal, 1931.

Chapter 9

1. Wright, "History of the San Diego River," 1:2–5.

2. Cosgrove, "Opinion."

3. Hundley, *Great Thirst*, 51, 58, 128, 130, 197; Cosgrove, "Opinion," 8, 12, 14, 22–23.

4. Hutchins, *Water Rights in the Nineteen Western States*, 156–57, 148.

5. "Oldest Records Show City's Right to San Diego River," *San Diego Union*, January 6, 1914, 5; "Human Nature and Law," *San Diego Sun*, January 6, 1914, 4.

6. "Answer of Applicant Ed Fletcher to the Protest of the City of San Diego," February 23, 1923, Fletcher Papers, UCSD Collection, Box 62, Folder 3.

7. Higgins, *This Fantastic City San Diego*, 5.

8. "City Attorney Satisfied with El Capitan Outcome," *San Diego Union*, March 31, 1918, 10.

9. "Council to Insist On Water Rights in Resolution," *San Diego Union*, October 14, 1921, Sec. II, 1.

10. Letter, Crouch to Fletcher, December 18, 1922, Fletcher Collection, Box 9, File 13; letter, Fletcher to Huber, September 6, 1921, Fletcher Collection, Box 9, File 8; letter, Fletcher to Freeman, August 16, 1923, Fletcher Collection, Box 9, File 15; letter, DeChant to Fletcher, March 15, 1923, Fletcher Collection, Box 9, File 14.

11. Higgins, *This Fantastic City San Diego*, 40; Wright, "History of the San Diego River," 2:227.

Chapter 10

1. "Council Opens Inquiry into Dam Conditions," *San Diego Union*, July 9, 1932.
2. For examples, see Ten-Day Reports in Pyle, *Feature History*, vol. 6.
3. Memo, Labor Inspector Knott to Savage, October 20, 1934, in Pyle, *Feature History*, 2:1,141.
4. Letter, Dan Rossi to Mayor, September 19, 1932, in Pyle, *Feature History*, 2:1,112, and letter, Savage to Mayor, September 21, 1932, in Pyle, *Feature History*, 2:1,113; "The Candidates Speak," *Opportunity*, November 1932, 338.
5. "Goeddel Halts Dam Payments Pending Labor Investigations," *San Diego Union*, September 7, 1932; "El Capitan Authority Given Up by Goeddel; Savage to Be in Charge," *San Diego Union*, September 17, 1932.
6. Letter, Ramon Ames and Bob Quitac to the Mayor and Council, December 21, 1931, in Pyle, *Feature History*, 5:2,802; letter, Savage to Mayor and Council, December 29, 1931, in Pyle, *Feature History*, 5:2,803; memo, Harold Wood, Resident Engineer to Savage, October 21, 1932, in Pyle, *Feature History*, 5:2,812–13.
7. "El Capitan Dedicated with Ceremony," *San Diego Union*, February 23, 1935, in Pyle, *Feature History*, 5:3,099.

Epilogue

1. "San Diego Launches Major Cleanup Effort for River," *San Diego Union*, December 14, 2017, B17; "Partnership Cleaning Up San Diego River," *San Diego Union*, July 12, 2018, B4A.

BIBLIOGRAPHY

Government Documents and Publications

Board of Engineers for Rivers and Harbors, U.S. Army Corps of Engineers, War Department. "The Port of San Diego." Washington, D.C.: Government Printing Office, 1955.

Bolton, Herbert Eugene, ed. *Historical Memoirs of New California by Father Francisco Palou*. 4 vols. Berkeley: University of California Press, 1926.

California State Department of Public Works. "San Diego County Investigation." *Bulletin No. 48*, Division of Water Resources, 1935.

California State Railroad Commission. "San Diego River Riparian Problem Resulting from Increasing the Supply of Cuyamaca Water Company." Report to Chairman John M. Eshlman by Charles H. Lee, September 16, 1912. George Cromwell Company, Engineering Reports on San Diego Water Supply. Exhibit "E."

City of Los Angeles v. City of San Fernando, 14 Cal. 3d. 199.

City of San Diego v. The Cuyamaca Water Company, 209 Cal. 151.

Colonel Ed Fletcher Collection. San Diego History Center Document Collection, MS 135, Series XVII.

Cosgrove, T.B. "An Opinion on the Rights of the City of San Diego to the Waters of the San Diego River." January 1914. San Diego, CA: E.P. Wilson Printers, 1914.

Cuyamaca Water Company Records. Special Collections and Archives, University of California, San Diego, MSS 0503.

Davidson, George. "Report of the Superintendent of the Coastal Survey, 1858." Washington, D.C.: William A. Harris Printing, 1859.

———. *United States Coastal Survey, Pacific Coast: Coastal Pilot of California, Oregon and Washington Territory*. Washington, D.C.: Government Printing Office, 1869.

Ed Fletcher Papers. Special Collections and Archives, University of California, San Diego, MSS 81.

Ellis, Arthur J., and Charles H. Lee. "Geology and Ground Water of the Western Part of San Diego County, California." U.S. Geological Survey, Paper 446. Washington, D.C.: Government Printing Office, 1919.

Freeman, John R. "Freeman Report: Summary of the Recommendations Regarding Future Extensions of Water Supply for the City of San Diego." May 1924. Ed Fletcher Papers, Special Collections and Archives, University of California, San Diego, MSS 81.

George H. Derby Collection, 1931–69. California Historical Society Collection, San Francisco, California.

Goudey, R.F., Assistant Engineer. "Investigation of the Water Supply at San Diego." Special Report No. 253. State of California, Bureau of Sanitary Engineering, January 14, 1921.

Hall, William Hammond. *Irrigation in Southern California*. 2 vols. Sacramento, CA: State Office of Printing, 1888.

Isray, James. *Sailing Directions for the West Coast of North America*. London: James Isray, 1853.

John S. Eastwood Papers. Special Collections and University Archives, University of California, Riverside, Water Resources Collection Archive.

Lanier, Bartlett, ed. *On the Old West Coast: Being the Reminiscences of a Ranger, by Major Horace Bell*. New York: William Morrow & Company, 1930.

Lux v. Haggin, 69 Cal 255 (1886).

McGlashan, H.D., and F.G. Ebert. "Southern California Floods of January 1916." Water Supply Paper 426. U.S. Geological Survey, Department of the Interior, in cooperation with the State of California. Washington, D.C.: Government Printing Office, 1918.

Palou, Fray Francisco. *Historical Memoirs of New California*. 4 vols. Translated and edited by Herbert E. Bolton. Berkeley: University of California Press, 1926.

Port of San Diego, California. *The Board of Engineers for Rivers and Harbors, War Department, Corps of Engineers, U.S. Army*. Washington, D.C.: Government Printing Office, 1955.

Pyle, Fred D. *Feature History: El Capitan Dam, 1931–35*. 6 vols. City of San Diego, 1935.

Records of the Chief of Engineers. National Archives and Records Administration, RG 77.

San Diego Chamber of Commerce. Minutes of the Regular and Executive Minutes of the Board of Directors. Manpower Library, San Diego, California.

San Diego County Water Authority. First Annual Report, 1946. San Diego, California.

———. "Groundwater Report," June 1997. Water Resources Department.

Secretary of War, Department of War. *Annual Reports of the Chief of Engineers*. Washington, D.C.: Government Printing Office, n.d.

State of California, Public Works Department. "San Diego County Investigation." *Bulletin #48*. Division of Water Resources, 1935.

———. "San Dieguito and San Diego River Investigation." *Bulletin #35*. Division of Water Resources, 1949.

Teggart, Frederick J., ed. *The Portola Expedition of 1769–1770: Diary of Miguel Costanso*. Berkeley: University of California Press, 1911.

U.S. Congress. *Memoir of the San Diego River*, by Lieutenant George H. Derby, House Document #1, Part III, 33rd Congress, 1st Session, 1853.

———. *Report of the United States and Mexico Boundary Survey of 1846*, by Major William H. Emory, 29th Congress, 1st Session, 1846.

———. *Report to Col. J.J. Abert, Chief of the Topographical Engineers*, April 30, 1853, Part III, Appendix E, in the Message from the President of the United States to the Both Houses of Congress. March 30, 1853.

U.S. Congress, House. *Conservation and Storage of Water, San Diego Cal., Hearings Before the House Committee of Public Lands*. HR 4037, 65th Congress, 2nd Session. Washington, D.C.: Government Printing Office, 1918.

———. *Examination and Survey of San Diego Harbor, Cal.*, by Lieutenant Colonel C.S. McKinstry, #1309. 62nd Congress, 3rd Session, 1912.

U.S. Congress, Senate. *Coast Survey Showing the Progress of the Survey During the Year 1858*, by Alexander Bache, #14, 35th Congress, 2nd Session, 1858.

United States Statutes at Large, 1789–2010. 124 vols. Washington, D.C.: Government Printing Office, 2010.

Vernon Irrigation Company v. City of Los Angeles, 106 Cal 237 (1895).

Winter v. United States, 207 US 564 (1908).

Wray, Christopher. *Notes of the San Diego Flume from Original Plans and Testimonies*. La Mesa, CA: Helix Water District, 1999.

Secondary Sources

Abbott, Patrick. *The Rise and Fall of San Diego*. San Diego, CA: Sunbelt Publications, 1999.

Adema, Thomas J. *Our Hills and Valleys: A History of the Helix-Spring Valley Region*. San Diego, CA: San Diego Historical Society, 1993.

Arax, Mark. *The Dreamt Land*. New York: Alfred A. Knoft, 2019.

Bancroft, Hubert Howe. *The History of California*. 6 vols. San Francisco, CA: A.L. Bancroft & Company, 1884.

Billington, David P., and Donald C. Jackson. *Big Dams of the New Deal Era: A Confluence of Engineering and Politics*. Norman: University of Oklahoma Press, 1991.

Black, Samuel F. *History of San Diego County*. 2 vols. Chicago: S.J. Clarke Publishing Company, 1913.

Carle, David. *Introduction to Water in California*. Berkeley: University of California Press, 2015.

Cleland, Robert Glass. *California: The American Period*. New York: Macmillan Company, 1939.

Crawford, Richard. *The Way We Were in San Diego*. Charleston, SC: The History Press, 2011.

Davis, Edward J.P. *Historical San Diego: The Birth Place of California*. San Diego, CA: Pioneer Press, 1953.

Dixon, Ben F. *Diario: The Journal of Padre Serra*. San Diego, CA: Don Diego's Libreria, 1964.

Englehart, Father Zephyrin. *San Diego Mission*. San Francisco, CA: James H. Barry Company, 1920.

Engstrand, Iris W. *San Diego: California's Cornerstone*. Tulsa, OK: Continental Press, 1980.

Fetzer, Leland. *The Cuyamacas: The Story of the San Diego's High County*. San Diego, CA: Sunbelt Publishing, 2008.

Fleck, John. *Water Is for Fighting For, and Other Myths about Water and the West*. Washington, D.C.: Overland Press, 2016.

Fletcher, Ed. *Memoirs*. San Diego, CA: Pioneer Printers, 1952.

Ford, Larry R. *Metropolitan San Diego*. Philadelphia: University of Pennsylvania Press, 2005.

Gleason, Duncan. *The Islands and Ports of California*. New York: Devin-Adair Company, 1958.

Green, Frederick M. "Safe Yield Study of the Complete Development of the Waters of the San Diego River, Surface and Underground, January

7, 1929." Report, Ed Fletcher Papers. Special Collections and Archives, University of California, San Diego, MSS 81, Box 37, Folder 3.

—————. *San Diego Old Mission Dam and Irrigation System.* Typed report. San Diego, CA: City Water Utilities Department, 1933.

Griswold, Richard Del Castillo. *The Treaty of Guadalupe-Hidalgo: A Legacy of Conflict.* Norman: University of Oklahoma Press, 1910.

Guinn, J.M. *A History of California and an Extended History of the Southern Counties.* 2 vols. Los Angeles, CA: The Historical Record Company, 1907.

Gumprecht, Blake. *The Los Angeles River: Its Life, Death, and Possible Rebirth.* Baltimore, MD: Johns Hopkins University Press, 1999.

Gunn, Douglas. *Picturesque San Diego with Historical and Descriptive Notes.* Chicago: Knight & Leonard Company Printing, 1886.

Harlow, Neal. *Maps of the Pueblo Lands of San Diego, 1602–1874.* Los Angeles, CA: Dawson Book Shop, 1987.

Hays, Samuel P. *Conservation and the Gospel of Efficiency: The Progressive Conservation Movement, 1890–1920.* Princeton, NJ: Princeton University Press, 1960.

Heilbron, Carl H. *The History of San Diego County.* 2 vols. San Diego, CA: San Diego Press Club, 1936.

Helix Water District. "Fast Flume Facts." N.P., 2012.

Hertlein, L.G., and U.S. Grant IV. "The Geology and Paleontology of the Marine Pliocene of San Diego County." *Memoirs of the San Diego Society of Natural History* 2 (August 1944): 23–32.

Higgins, Shelley. *This Fantastic City San Diego.* San Diego, CA: City of San Diego, 1956.

Hopkins, Harry C. *The History of San Diego: Its Land and Water.* San Diego, CA: City Printing Company, 1929.

Hundley, Norris. *Dividing the Waters: A Century of Controversy Between the United States and Mexico.* Berkeley: University of California Press, 1966.

—————. *The Great Thirst, Californians and Water: A History.* Berkeley: University of California Press, 2001.

—————. *Water and the West: The Colorado River Compact and the Politics of Water in the American West.* Berkeley: University of California Press, 1975.

Hutchins, Wells A. *California Law of Water Rights.* Sacramento: State Engineer of California, 1956.

—————. *Water Rights in the Nineteen Western States.* 2 vols. Washington, D.C.: Government Printing Office, 1974.

Igler, David. "When Is a River Not a River: Reclaiming Nature's Disorder in Lux v Haggin." *Environmental History* 1, no. 2 (April 1996): 52–69.

Ingram, B. Lynn, and Malamud-Roan Frances. *The West without Water: What Past Floods, Droughts, and Other Climate Clues Tell Us About Tomorrow*. Berkeley: University of California Press, 2013.

Innis, Jack Scheffler. *San Diego's Legends: The Events, People and Places that Made History*. San Diego, CA: Sunbelt Publications, 2004.

Isenberg, Andrew C. *Mining California: An Ecological History*. New York: Hill and Wang, 2005.

Jackson, Donald C. *Building the Ultimate Dam: John S. Eastwood and the Control of Water in the West*. Lawrence: University of Kansas Press, 1995.

Kaufmann, Obi. *The State of Water: Understanding California's Most Precious Resource*. Berkeley: University of California Press, 1990.

Kelley, Robert. *Battling the Inland Sea: Floods, Public Policy, and the Sacramento Valley*. Berkeley: University of California Press, 1998.

Kittle, Robert A. *Franciscan Frontiersmen: How Three Adventurers Charted the West*. Norman: University of Oklahoma, 2017.

McGrew, Clarence A. *The City of San Diego and San Diego County: The Birth Place of California*. 2 vols. Chicago: American Historical Society, 1922.

McWilliams, Carey. *California the Great Exception*. Berkeley: University of California Press, 1999.

Morrison, Patt, and Mark Lamonica. *Rio L.A.: Tales from the Los Angeles River*. Los Angeles, CA: Angel City Press, 2001.

Mount, Jeffrey. *California Rivers and Streams: The Conflict Between Fluvial Process and Land Use*. Berkeley: University of California Press, 1995.

Perry, James I. *History of the Development of the San Diego Water Supply*. City of San Diego, CA: Public Utility Department, 1965.

Phillips, Irene. *Six Historical Sketches*. San Diego, CA: South Bay Press, 1960.

Phoenixiana: A Collection of the Burlesques & Sketches of John Phoenix, Alias, John P. Squibob, Who Was, in Fact, George H. Derby. San Francisco, CA: Grabhorn Press, 1937. Originally published, New York: D. Appleton & Company, 1856.

Pourade, Richard. *The History of San Diego*. 7 vols. San Diego, CA: Union-Tribune Publishing Company, 1960–77.

Pryde, Philip R. *San Diego: An Introduction to the Region*. San Diego, CA: Sunbelt Publications, 1976.

Reiser, Marc. *Cadillac Desert*. New York: Viking Penguin Press, 1986.

San Diego County Water Authority. *To Quench a Thirst*. City of San Diego, CA: self-published, 2005.

Sax, John L. *Legal Control of Water Resources*. St. Paul, MO: Thompson and West, 2006.

Schubert, Frank N., ed. *The Nation Builders: A Sesquicentennial History of the Corps of Topographical Engineers, 1838–1863*. Fort Belvour, VA: Office of History, U.S. Army Corps of Engineers, 1888.

Shipek, Florence C. *Pushed into the Rocks: Southern California Indian Land Tenure, 1769–1986*. Lincoln: University of Nebraska Press, 1988.

Smith, Walter Gifford. *The Story of San Diego*. San Diego, CA: City Publishing Company, 1892.

Smythe, William E. *The Conquest of Arid America*. New York: McMillan & Company, 1899.

———. *The History of San Diego, 1542–1908*. San Diego, CA: History Company, 1908.

Starr, Kevin. *American and the California Dream, 1850–1915*. New York: Oxford University Press, 1986.

Steward, Donald M. *Frontier Port: A Chapter in San Diego's History*. Los Angeles, CA: W. Ritchie Press, 1965.

Turhollow, Anthony F. *A History of the Los Angeles District, U.S. Army Corps of Engineers, 1898–1965*. Los Angeles, CA: U.S. Army Engineering District, 1975.

Tyler, Daniel. *The Mythical Pueblo Rights Doctrine: Water Administration in Hispanic New Mexico*. El Paso: Texas Western Press, 1990.

Ward, Russell E. "About Santee & Me." Santee Historical Society Collection.

Weber, F. Harold. *Mines and Mineral Resources of San Diego County, California*. San Francisco: California Division of Mines, 1963.

Worester, Donald. *Rivers of Empire*. New York: Oxford University Press, 1992.

Wright, William L. "The History of the San Diego River." 2 vols. Unpublished typed transcript, 1933.

Articles

Beerman, Paul. "El Capitan Dam Spillway." *Municipal Employee*, February 1933, 3–5.

City of San Diego. "Mission Valley Groundwater Aquifer." Water Resources Division, 2020.

Dixon, Ben F. "Documents of San Diego History." *Journal of San Diego History* 10, no. 3 (July 1964): 40–42.

Engstrand, Iris W. "Pietro Fages and Miguel Costanso: Two Letters from San Diego in 1769." *Journal of San Diego History* 21, no. 2 (Spring 1975): 1–11.

Farley, Bill. "The Cuyamaca Water Company Partnership: New Scenes from San Diego's Water History." *Journal of San Diego History* 62, no. 2 (Spring 2016): 181–202.

Farquhar, Francis P. "Topographical Reports of Lieutenant George H. Derby." *California Historical Society Quarterly* 11 (June 1932): 99–123.

Fire Engineering 49, no. 20. "Water System for San Diego" (May 1911).

Gabridson, Ed. "Mission Bay Aquatic Park." *Journal of San Diego History* 48, no. 1 (Winter 2002): 38–47.

Garcia, Victor W. "El Cajon, California." *Journal of San Diego History* 30, no. 4 (Fall 1990): 221–33.

Hennessey, Greg. "The Politics of Water in San Diego, 1895–1897." *Journal of San Diego History* 24, no. 3 (Summer 1978): 367–83.

Hill, Joseph. "Dry Rivers, Dammed Rivers and Floods: An Early History of the Struggle Between Droughts and Floods in San Diego." *Journal of San Diego History* 48, no. 1 (Winter 2002): 48–59.

Hoyt, Frederick G. "Marketing a Booming City in 1887: San Diego and the Chicago Press." *Journal of San Diego History* 45, no. 2 (Spring 1999): 86–105.

ICF International. "Final Cultural Resources Inventory and Impact Assessment for the San Diego River Trail El Monte Segment Project." Prepared for the County of San Diego, August 2005.

Minan, John H. "The San Diego River: A Natural, Historical, and Recreational Resource." *San Diego Law Review* 41, no. 3 (2004): 1,139–76.

Mogilner, Geoffrey. "Cosoy: Birthplace of New California." *Journal of San Diego History* 62, no. 2 (Spring 2016): 131–58.

Patterson, Thomas W. "Hatfield the Rainmaker." *Journal of San Diego History* 16, no. 4 (Winter 1970): 3–32.

Pryde, Philip R. "The Day the San Diego River Was Saved: The History of Floods and Floodplain Planning in Mission Valley." *Journal of San Diego History* 57, no. 3 (September 2002): 154–84.

Pyle, Fred D. "The San Diego City Water Supply." *Municipal Employee* 4, no. 4 (October 1935): 1–4.

Randel, B.F. "Bringing the Colorado River to San Diego." *Professional Engineer* (December 1924): 7–9.

Ruscavage-Barz, Samantha, and Diane Albert. "Indian Reserved Water Rights." Report at the Western Governor's Association of the Western States Water Council, 1984.

San Diego Chamber of Commerce. "A River Won." *San Diego Magazine* (January 1931): 10–11, 16.

Sholders, Mike. "Water Supply Development in San Diego and a Review of Related Outstanding Projects." *Journal of San Diego History* 48, no. 1 (Winter 2002): 60–71.

Smith, Jeff. "San Diego's Five Worst Floods." *The Reader* (June 2003).

Strathman, Theodore. "Land, Water, and Real Estate: Ed Fletcher and the Cuyamaca Water Company, 1910–1926." *Journal of San Diego History* 50, no. 3 and 4 (Summer/Fall 2004): 124–44.

Thickens, Virginia, and Margaret Mollins. "Putting a Lid on California." *California Historical Society Quarterly* 31, no. 2 (1952): 221–33, 367–83.

Thorne, Tanis C. "The Removal of the Indians of El Capitan to Viejas: Confrontation and Change in San Diego Indians Affairs in the 1930s." *Journal of San Diego History* 56, no. 1 and 2 (Spring 2010): 43–66.

White, George H. "Sixty Years Uphill." *San Diego Magazine* (April 1930): 5–8.

Wueste, R.C. "The Impounding Works of the San Diego Water System." *Journal of the American Water Works Association* 18, no. 3 (September 1927): 300–309.

Unpublished Dissertations

Martin, Eliza L. "Growth by the Gallon: Development and Power in San Diego, California, 1890–1947." Doctoral diss., University of California–Santa Cruz, 2010.

Strathman, Theodore. "Dreams of a Big City: Water Politics and San Diego Growth, 1910–1947." Doctoral diss., University of California–San Diego, 2005.

Interviews

McGirr, Devan, Archivist, Barona Cultural Center and Museum, December 2017.

Pasek, Jeff, Watershed Manager, City of San Diego, November 2017 and September 2020.

Savage, Aline, resident of El Monte, California, September 2018.

Wray, Christopher. E-mail interview, 2017.

Oral History

Jennings, William H. Interviewed by Tom G. Hall, 1965. G4072 J7-3, Center for Oral History Research, University of California, Los Angeles. http://oralhistory.library.ucla.edu.

Newspapers and Collections

California Digital Newspaper Collection.
Engineering News.
Los Angeles Times.
Pacific Rural Press.
Professional Engineer.
San Diego Evening Tribune.
San Diego Herald.
San Diego Labor Leader.
San Diego Sun.
San Diego Union.
San Diego Union-Tribune.
San Diego Water Department Archive, Newspaper Scrapbook Collection.

INDEX

ABOUT THE AUTHOR

John Martin, a San Diego native, grew up near the river and spent many summer days cooling off in the water by the Old Mission Dam. He has a graduate degree in history; is a frequent contributor to the *Journal of San Diego History*, with articles ranging from San Diego military history to the development of the town's water infrastructure; and a regular presenter at the San Diego Congress of History.